Not Quite Your Typical

Stroke
BOOK!

Not Quite Your Typical

Stroke
BOOK!

OK, you have had your stroke; now how do you really live again?

MIKE DOSEMAGEN

Cover layout provided by 360 MediaGroup

Author photo provided by Mike Dosemagen

Page design by Win-Win Words LLC

ISBN: 978-0-692-19869-8

Printed in the United States of America

Contents

Preface

I HAD MY STROKE IN EARLY DECEMBER 2011. SOON AFTER I HAD THE STROKE, I determined that I would learn as much as possible about how it had affected me and what was in store for me. I read as many books about strokes as I could, while also researching the Internet. Most of the books I wanted to read had been published long before and were out of print, unavailable to me. Many of the books I did find were often written like textbooks, offering far too much detail for a typical stroke survivor to comprehend. Still other books had been authored by stroke survivors who had unlimited resources for rehabilitative therapy well beyond what most of us could afford. They certainly weren't written for the stroke survivors I was encountering.

Eventually, I found one book that was on a bookshelf

in an out-of-the-way room used by a support group, which meets at a major university in Tennessee and which I attend. This book was published in the 1990s; as I read it, I could see that much of it was very close to the experiences I encountered during my stroke. As I read it, I found myself actually reliving my stroke and experiencing many of the same sensations. I literally had to stop reading it at times due to this. Unfortunately, when I tried to purchase this book, it was out of print as well. No book stores in my area or most other markets stock books about strokes, so I completed an exhaustive internet search for this book.

So, I figured I would plug that gap by writing my own book, which is what you have here. I committed myself to writing a book about strokes that would be simple to understand and easily read by most people who had lost some but not all of their cognitive abilities. It is also intended to be read by a stroke survivor's caregivers and family members.

Finally, I wrote this as though I were sitting there having a conversation with you, the reader. While this is not the approach that I would normally use, I have found that speaking with people enhances their ability to grasp the subject.

I very seldom converse with anyone about my life and the many things I have done, so this style of writing was not easy for me at all. I tend to be a very introverted person, but I hope that this book will give you a good understanding of what you can expect as you recover from your stroke. It covers a lot of important but ignored subjects ranging from financial issues to how to get dressed to how to maintain a household.

I hope you learn that having a stroke doesn't have to be a negative experience, but it can have many positive aspects as well. I know that for me I would really have to think twice about going back to my "pre-stroke" life.

Not Quite Your Typical

Stroke
BOOK!

Chapter 1

The Big Event

FRIDAY, DECEMBER 2, 2011, WAS THE FIRST DAY OF WHAT WOULD BE MY "NEW" LIFE. That morning, my daughter Tami took me to a local emergency room, where it was diagnosed I was having a stroke.

Doctors determined that my stroke had been caused by a blood clot in the upper left side of my brain. The clot was about two and a half centimeters long and about a centimeter in diameter. It had started to form during the day on Thursday, December 1, 2011, and it took until Monday morning to reach its maximum size. It was also Monday morning that all of the physical effects started to take over as well.

Thursday morning had started out quite foggy in Hendersonville, Tennessee, with temperatures right around freezing. Early that morning there had been a major car accident on an overpass of Highway 386, our local bypass otherwise known as Vietnam Veterans Boulevard. It involved more than a hundred vehicles in a chain reaction that occurred on an icy overpass in the dense fog. The vehicles involved included two school buses as well as trucks, SUVs, and cars. There were multiple injuries and at least one fatality. Many emergency vehicles from all around the area responded. It took nearly the entire day to clear the roadway.

I would always drive my old Suburban to work when the weather was less than ideal, saving my Mustang for the sunny days. That Thursday morning I decided I would take the Suburban, and then that evening I was going to join Tami and my granddaughter Emma and some other family members to celebrate Emma's eighth birthday at Dave and Buster's in Nashville.

Thursday was a slow day at work, so every chance I had, I peeked online to find out what I could about the accident. At one time I had been a volunteer fireman in our community and always kept up with situations like this when I could.

The weather was such that day that we had no customers at the Chevrolet dealership at which I worked, so after my training and follow-up calls were done, it was a dull day. At lunch time I went to pick up something to eat. Occasionally, I found myself having trouble lifting up my right foot. I didn't think much about it, as I had been sitting all morning and was a bit tired and, quite frankly, bored.

That afternoon I kept following the accident. I got ahead on my training and just kept waiting for a customer to come in. I finally left work at 5:30 P.M., which was a half-hour early, so I could go get a card for Emma. I really felt funny, almost disoriented, and was having a hard time walking the three hundred or so feet to the car, but again I thought of it as being tired.

When I stopped to pick up the card, I was having even more trouble walking. When I got to Dave and Buster's, I almost dreaded going in, but getting to Emma's eighth birthday party was important to me. Tami's mother-in-law-to-be noticed I was stumbling around somewhat while walking, but I made it through the party and arrived back to my apartment without incident. On the trip home, I remember being thankful that I had my Suburban instead of having to shift the manual transmission in my Mustang. I went right to bed thinking when I woke up Friday morning, I would feel and function better. I really had nothing major planned for my day off Friday other than some work on my resumé, so I could take it relatively easy.

To the Hospital

On Friday morning I woke up at seven. I had a hard time getting my balance while getting out of bed, but my walking seemed to be better, and I felt much better. I watched the news, and at 7:30 I went into the bathroom to shower.

When I went to wash my hair, though, I could not raise my right arm to my head. That is when it became apparent to me that there was something seriously wrong.

I finished my shower by shaving and washing myself with my left hand. As soon as I got out of the shower, I called Tami and asked her to come and get me so she could take me to the hospital. I told her to take her time even though she suggested I call an ambulance. I reaffirmed to her to take her time as I needed to get dressed. During the half-hour it took her to get here, I got dressed, made the bed and even took out the garbage.

When Tami got to my apartment, I again went over what I was experiencing, and what I had done during the time she was driving over. We went to the hospital and the admissions nurse immediately suspected that I was having a stroke. Less than ten minutes after walking in the door, I was lying on an ER hospital bed. By this time, I could not fill out the admission forms with my right hand, and my speech was funny. The ER doctor confirmed the stroke and immediately began to take my vital signs and to draw a blood sample. My blood pressure and heart rate by this time were elevated to the point I could feel them slightly. My temperature and breathing were normal.

The ER doctor wanted to bring the blood pressure and heart rate down even though they were barely above normal ranges. By this time, I was beginning to realize this could be a major event. I was getting nervous and scared, which could be why my BP was higher than normal. The doctor, Tami, and I then went through the doctor's line of questioning about what I had eaten that morning, diabetes control, exercise, smoking, whether I drank liquor or not, what prescription drugs I was on, and other typical questions.

By the end of the ER doctor's questioning, we had established the following information: I had not yet eaten anything that morning. I am not a coffee drinker, but I had had a small amount of soda, which is normal for me. I have type II diabetes but have had it well under control by watching my diet for five years. I had a fulltime sedimentary job but usually did get up and walk or was on my feet quite a bit. I did get quite a bit of exercise doing physical work on my days off, so I kept myself in pretty good shape overall. I did smoke, but less than a pack a day. I was not on any prescription drugs; in fact, I had not even taken as much as an aspirin for several months. I was unaware of any allergic reactions to medications. I have clear lungs and no signs of heart problems from past physicals. I do not drink any alcohol, as my father was an alcoholic and I saw the negative effects of that in the past. My mother was nearly eighty when she died. She died of old age, but a stroke occurred as her body was shutting down. Basically, I was in good-to-above-average shape for being sixty-one years old.

After the questioning by the ER doctor was completed, he ordered some medication for me to reduce my blood pressure and heart rate. He also called for a brain CT scan.

There is medication available to attempt to treat the effects of a stroke when it has occurred. The drug is nowhere near effective 100 percent of the time and must be given within the first three to four hours or so from the time the stroke starts. In my case, that meant I should have had the drug administered Thursday morning, although what was I to know at the time? That was well before I even realized I had a real problem. Hindsight is 20-20.

The medication that the doctor ordered to reduce my blood pressure was Hydralazine HCl, which also is supposed to lower the heart rate. Before this drug was administered, my blood pressure's systolic reading (the top number) was 140 to 145. Within ten minutes of the injection, however, I could feel both my blood pressure and heart rate rising. There also was a definite warming sensation starting in my legs and working upward into my abdomen. No question: I was having a severely adverse reaction to the drug.

Tami went to get the doctor, and by the time he got back, my systolic blood pressure was approaching 200 and my heart was beating like crazy. Unfortunately, all that anyone can do at that point in terms of treating the adverse effects of the Hydralazine HCl was to let the BP and pulse come down on their own over time. The CT scan was delayed until my blood pressure and heart rate were somewhat stabilized. I tried to keep comfortable and relax for the next hour so my blood pressure would drop.

In late morning, I was taken into radiology for the CT scan, even though my blood pressure had not fully stabilized. Once inside the room where the CT scan was to be performed, I was not allowed to move from the ER bed onto the scanner table alone; rather, I was moved by the nursing staff. That was quite an interesting task, as the CT scanner room was a bit small—not a lot of room to maneuver. I obviously had to keep my head from moving during the CT scan and did so quite well. After the CT scan, I was transferred back onto the ER bed and wheeled back to the room in the ER.

I spent the next couple of hours in ER just resting and allowing my blood pressure to come down, which it was doing very slowly. It was still high, well above normal range—even what was normal for me. Seeing this, the ER doctor told Tami and me that it would probably be sometime in the evening before my numbers would be back to normal. He also told us that he was waiting for a room to become available for me to move into, at which time I would be officially admitted. I remember thinking how boring it was lying there, not doing anything, and that I should be doing something else.

In the middle of the afternoon that Friday, I was moved upstairs to a room. Once I got comfortable, I must have gone into a deep sleep. Tami later told me that while I was sleeping, she went down to the cafeteria to get something to eat, and when she came back up to the room I was lying on the floor. Apparently, I had gotten up in my sleep to go to the bathroom and had fallen. I have no recollection of that happening.

I woke up Saturday morning, and Tami was still there. She had spent the night in what must have been an uncomfortable chair. (She did this for several days, and I was quite thankful to have her there.) Later that morning, my neurologist stopped by to introduce himself. He had me push against his arm with each leg, twist both feet, squeeze his hand with my right hand, and show him the range of motion in my right arm. To me, my legs felt OK, but my right arm showed some weakness and lack of motion. I could also tell that, when I smiled, the right side of my mouth felt like it was not moving as far as the left, and my speech was becoming more affected.

An Evolving Stroke

The neurologist explained that I was experiencing an evolving stroke; we would have to wait a day or two longer to see how badly I was going to be affected. He explained that every stroke was different, but they often had similarities. In my case, I had developed a blood clot in the upper left side of my brain. The left side of the brain controls the right side of the body and vice versa. The blood clot was fully blocking the blood vessels where it had developed, therefore preventing blood flow in the vessels beyond the clot. This is the area of the brain that controlled much of the muscle structure on my right side. Without proper blood flow, part of my brain had essentially been killed. Anyone who had ever accused me of being brain dead was now at least partially right.

I also was told that eventually the blood could seek an alternate path around the clot and I would regain some muscle control. The brain can be a marvelous thing in restoring injuries, and it was entirely possible that it would create a detour for the blood flow. Surgery to remove the clot was not a common practice as the risks of further permanent damage were way too high in my case. The absolute best way to treat the stroke was to let it run its course and concentrate on rehabilitation. Another point he made was that approximately 90 percent of my ultimate total recovery would occur within the first year.

The last thing the neurologist wanted to know was if I was aware that I had had five previous mini-strokes, or TIAs, which are transient ischemic attacks. I told him I could remember my right hand going numb a few times over the past few years, but those events were after long days of hard physical yard work. They would go away after a few minutes and my drinking a good amount of water. I had assumed the numbness was from being somewhat dehydrated. He explained those events were the mini-strokes. He also said that what I did was what most people would have thought and done.

Long Hours

I had been spending a lot of time working at the dealership fifty to fifty-five hours a week and working at my part-time floor-cleaning business whenever I could. By the beginning of November 2011, I had realized that there had been only one day in October when I hadn't worked at least five hours and on some days as much as fourteen hours. I started to slow down with work somewhat, and in November I had taken off two or three full days where I didn't do any work. I had seen signs that the economy was improving and had developed a plan to seek more lucrative employment. I had begun to update my resumé in the evenings as time permitted. I was determined to make 2012 a much better year for me, and on that Friday my goal was to finalize my resumé and begin an online job search.

After my neurologist left the room, I started to think about how hard I had been working. I went through the thought process of what I had been doing to myself and ended up realizing that the stroke was God's way of telling me that he was going to make sure I was going to take a vacation. I was going to come out of this situation alive and relatively well. As soon as I came to that realization, my thoughts became not to worry about the past, but to concentrate on my new career, with that being the best possible stroke recovery.

During the rest of Saturday, Tami called my employer and told them what had happened and that I would not be at work for a while. For lunch at the hospital, I was given a meal and soft drink but ate very little. I just plain did not have the appetite for much food. Tami went down to the cafeteria after I promised not to get up. The balance of the day was spent with visitors and periodic naps.

On Sunday morning I was visited by my neurologist's brother, who was also a neurologist. We went through the same physical tests. I had lost control just as my neurologist expected. Tami went to my apartment and got some clothing of mine, as well as my toothbrush and toiletries, to bring to me in the hospital. She also picked up the book that I had been reading. The visitor count slowed, and overall it was a slow, restful day. I learned that not too much takes place in the hospital on Sundays, unless of course there is an emergency situation.

Rehab Starts Now

On Monday morning, things picked up a bit. My personal physician stopped by and suggested a couple of options regarding rehab facilities, as rehabilitation would be at a different hospital facility. She also went through with me what had happened, and she was pleased to know that I had my neurologist and his brother caring for me. She told me that she would, of course, stay in touch with them and be available for any questions I might have. She approved of the medications that had been prescribed, and reiterated what the neurologist had told me about the stroke overall.

My neurologist stopped by again and repeated the physical tests. By this time, I had lost even more strength and muscle control from the stroke, although he explained it would probably not get any worse, as it had evolved to the maximum. Over the next two days, he said, he would schedule a full-body MRI and repeat the CT scan of my brain.

A woman from hospital administration came up a bit later and we discussed where I would like to go for rehabilitation therapy. There were several facilities in the area. The one that was rated the best was a sister hospital that was also near my home and more convenient for Tami. The other one was in the center of Nashville and not as convenient to me. I decided on the first option. Part of my thinking was I would be close to home and maybe get myself there. But that was a really goofy idea because I wasn't going anywhere for several months. Still, I wanted to be as close to home as possible. Now it became a matter of room availability, which could take a few days.

On Tuesday, four days after going to the hospital, I was visited by my neurologist. He told me that I would be given the CT scan of my brain on Wednesday. He had been in contact with my physician, and they concluded that I would also be given a full-body MRI scan to make sure I was not subject to any further problems. This was to make sure that my heart, lungs, and circulatory system were functioning properly and would not contribute to further problems. This was reassuring, as I wanted to get well, not look forward to more problems.

The two tests were completed on Wednesday. The MRI was a real trip. When I was transferred to the machine, the technician discussed with me what I could expect. It would be noisy inside the machine, and I could not move. It would also take about twenty minutes. She wanted to know if I was claustrophobic because many people do have issues dealing with the confinement. I used the experience to take a short nap. It was like the CT scan but took quite a bit longer because they scanned my whole body instead of just my shoulders and above.

On Thursday morning the lady from administration came back to begin the process of getting me discharged. Moving day had finally arrived! She would be back later with all the discharge paperwork. My neurologist also stopped in to see me and to go over the results of the CT scan. There were no indications of further damage. While I had a long way to go, I could expect no more problems through the rehab process. It would take time, though, and I would most likely never return to be 100 percent normal.

The first year was going to be the toughest. He reiterated that whatever recovery I was able to make in the first twelve months would be about what I could expect overall. Anything beyond twelve months would be small and very incremental. Finally, my personal physician stopped by and discussed the MRI results. There were no indications of any further physical problems anyplace else from the MRI. My heart, lungs, and circulatory system were all strong and normal or better than normal for a sixty-one-year-old man.

I was given my discharge papers on Thursday afternoon and was handed an eighty-page booklet discussing the known causes and highlights of causes and rehabilitation from strokes. I have to admit here that I only glanced at the book and didn't really read it for several months.

Later that afternoon, I was given a ride in an ambulance to the other hospital that was going to be my rehab home for the next three weeks. This was my first time ever riding in an ambulance. I got to sit up on the gurney and look out the rear window at Tami following behind in her car. That poor kid had been by my side almost since I was admitted. I not only appreciated it, but I also knew she needed to get home and relax in her own environment. It took a little over fifteen minutes of travel time to get to the second hospital.

The next phase of my new life was about to begin.

Chapter 2
Inpatient Therapy

THE NEXT HOSPITAL I WENT TO WAS NICE. It had been built only three or four years earlier, and my room was very nice. The first room I stayed in was on the third floor and located right across from the Rehab Gym, and there was a lot of activity on the floor. The staff there was every bit as helpful and polite as the staff at the first hospital had been, and I felt right at home, considering. Tami had left for the evening, so I was really on my own. I had not been sleeping all that well, but I slept very well the first night at the second hospital.

Early in the morning, a nice lady paid me a visit and introduced herself as my rehabilitation physician. She explained that I would be having three sessions a day of rehab therapy, five days a week. Therapy sessions were scheduled Monday through Friday, meaning I would have weekends "off." I would have therapy in three areas—physical, occupational, and speech. Each session would be about an hour long, encompassing a total of three hours a day. The first few sessions would be to determine what capabilities were lost and to plan the best approach going forward.

Shortly before nine in the morning, I was taken by wheelchair into the gym for breakfast. I was pretty excited to be wheeled out of that room, as I had been pretty much confined to and isolated in my room at the first hospital. The gym was a room measuring about fifty feet by forty feet. At one end there was equipment for physical therapy, while the equipment for occupational therapy was closer to the windows. A kitchen and two tables occupied the remaining area, which comprised about a quarter of the room.

The kitchen was used for serving breakfast to six or eight patients. Most of the breakfast had been prepared ahead of time in the hospital kitchen; however, a few patients had special menu items prepared in the gym. I really can't remember what I had, but there was a lot of French toast, sausage, and thickened liquids available. By this time, the menu sure sounded good to me. In fact, anything edible looked good to me as I had not been eating much.

I was in a group of six people that first day. As I looked around, I saw one gentleman who looked like he was about my age. I asked him, "What are you in here for?" I couldn't understand his response, but I later learned that he had been undergoing rehab from a major auto accident and had improved enough to where he was being discharged that weekend. It turns out the rehab center was for all types of brain injuries, not just stroke victims. In fact, most of the people there had been admitted there as the result of major brain injuries from other causes.

Intro to Therapy

Later in the day I was returned to the gym for physical therapy. The therapist there had heard me in the morning when I had questioned the other gentleman about why he was in there. She and some of the other therapists thought my understated and somewhat sarcastic sense of humor might help some of the others, many of whom felt doomed in there. During the time I was there, most of the patients in therapy were having difficulty with more than just one arm and one leg, which is what I was dealing with—I was better off than the others in that regard. As much as I appreciated being there, I felt terrible for most of the other patients who were in far worse condition than I was. Many of the patients were merely waiting for a room in the appropriate nursing home or assisted-living facility to open up for them.

During breakfast the first day, I quickly learned that the sealed tops of the various containers for syrup, butter, and beverages presented new obstacles. Normally, when these are opened, you hold with one hand and peel off the lid with the other. It is easy to do with two functioning hands, which makes it a very effective packaging technique. Performing this simple chore with only one useful hand, however, requires a different technique. Essentially, you open this type of container by using the palm and assistance from two fingers to hold the container to the table while peeling the top back with the two other fingers of the same hand. This technique worked well for the syrup and juice containers, but a more delicate method was needed for the butter and jam because they were much smaller. After a few days, I was able to maneuver these containers successfully and get them opened. The next step was getting the butter out. Eventually, I learned to hold butter knives by the blade with my thumb and forefinger, hold the container with the remaining fingers, and pop the butter out of the container. It took a couple of days, but I soon got used to opening these containers successfully. The most frustrating part was the amount of time and concentration it took.

I quickly learned the form of treatment for each of the three types of therapy, all of which were necessary for my recovery. Much of what each of the therapists did in treating me involved more than just the name given to each particular form of therapy. The speech therapist had the hardest assignment. She was responsible for making sure that I could not only speak well, but that I could swallow properly, eat properly, think properly, and communicate my thoughts. Not only did I have individual therapy with her, but she was in charge of those involved in the breakfast group as well. It took me nearly two weeks to realize that she had this much responsibility.

After breakfast on Monday morning, my rehab physician arranged for a visit to the radiology department to check my ability to swallow. This obviously is a vital function to sustaining life. I was given several thickened liquids with dyes in them to see how I was swallowing. We did the same with small amounts of food as well. I was able to pass this test, but, as a precaution, was kept on thickened liquids for a few more days. I was able to see the actions in my throat during the swallowing process and was quite impressed with the mechanics of it. I continued with the breakfast group for ten days. After that, I was deemed OK to eat in my room with the progress that I had made with that aspect of my recovery.

Frustration

I quickly became frustrated with speech therapy, though. I was having to repeat the list of, first, one-syllable words, then progressing to two-syllable words, then three-syllable words, and then phrases. Because of this slow progression by her design, going over and over the same drill, I started to feel like she wasn't giving me enough credit for the progress I believed I was making. Finally, I explained to her that I thought I could do better than just recite words to her. Tami had brought my laptop to the hospital, so I spent much of my time in my room on Facebook and reading email. I was also starting a diary of what my progress was with each therapist each day. At one point I managed to ask my speech therapist if I could get extra credit by setting up a spreadsheet for her personal budget the next day. She agreed to try that the next day.

The next morning the speech therapist and I held our session in my room with the laptop out. I began to set up an Excel spreadsheet for her similar to my personal budgeting spreadsheet. I had developed this about ten years before. I explained to her that with my spreadsheet, I could go back and see how much I had spent on monthly bills and major expenses for that entire time. Ditto my income for that whole period. Well, that session pretty much ended my daily speech therapy; I demonstrated that I had not lost any of my mental capabilities. I reasoned that she had originally assessed my capabilities as similar to most of the other patients there—patients who were in much worse shape than I was. By the end of that session we had developed a mutual respect and understanding of one another.

Wheelchair 101

Then there was my physical therapy. It involved restoring my ability to use my legs, for which I would spend an hour a day in the gym five days a week. The first thing I learned was how to get into a wheelchair with the assistance of not only the therapist, but also other hospital staffers. This became my standard method of travel throughout the hospital.

Learning how to maneuver my way into and out of the wheelchair really required a whole lot of learning. I was accustomed to getting into office chairs that rolled, but this in no way was the same as getting into a wheelchair. I eventually learned that the brakes had to be set on *both* wheels before I sat into or got out of the wheelchair. That was the most important thing of all, as a wheelchair has this annoying knack of rolling out from under you while you are getting into it or out of it. This is especially true when you have limited capability due to a right leg and arm that were essentially nonfunctional.

Wheelchairs also have footrests on front. These can be turned sideways to the outside or rotated from their normal position to the outside, away from where your legs go. Either way you do it, they have to be placed out of the way so the user can get into or out of a wheelchair. Maneuvering the footrests out of the way was impossible for me at first, so I was totally dependent on help to get me into the wheelchair. As much as I wanted to get into and out of the chair by myself, I really needed the assistance at first. Of course, I was hard headed and wanted to show these people here how determined I was to reach my goal of independence. Yeah, right.

As my physical therapy progressed, my therapist would have me move the wheelchair by myself. She would take me into the hallway and get the footrests out of the way for me, and then she would have me push the wheelchair with just my left leg. There was no way I could get my left foot to pull the chair forward, so I had to use my foot to push it backward. At first, I could move the chair backward about six inches at a time. I really never was able to get much better than that, but I looked at it this way: even eight inches is a 33 percent improvement over six inches.

The floors at this second hospital for me were vinyl tile laid on top of concrete, which is not as flat as you might think when poured and finished. If the concrete is within an eighth or three-sixteenths of an inch of being level (perfectly flat), that is a really good job. You rarely can see these surface fluctuations of concrete when walking, riding a bike, roller skating, skate boarding, or any other normal uses. But think about it: you *can* see the differences when small puddles form on patios, garage floors, driveways, or even basement floors. This is the kind of thing you notice when you have spent as much time as I did trying to negotiate surfaces in the condition I was in. I'll tell you what, when I was pushing that wheelchair backward along that concrete with my left foot, it felt like I was trying to pedal a bicycle up a mountain. It was agonizingly difficult going up those slight rises. Of course, as hard as it was going up the rises, going down them was like riding a bike and coasting down a steep slope. When you are recovering from a debilitating stroke, you learn to appreciate whatever victories and conveniences you can experience in your newfound life. This was my "new normal," albeit with my determination to keep improving.

There was no way I could use my right arm against the right wheel to move the chair. In fact, the wheelchair the hospital assigned to me had a padded tray affixed to the right arm to make it more comfortable for that arm. In addition, the tray kept my arm from falling into the right wheel and becoming further injured. Of course, this tray made it more difficult for me to get into and out of the chair. It was just another obstacle. When I would use only my left hand to move the left wheel, the chair would only turn to the right. In other words, there was no way to use my left arm and hand to move the chair any distance. I became very dependent on others for most of my mobility.

The Hemi Walker

As I continued on in physical therapy, I learned to use a device called a hemi walker. It is a metal, four-legged walking device with rubber nubs at the bottom of each leg where the leg meets the floor. Each pair of legs meet and are joined at the top, connected by a horizontal handle which the patient (like me) uses to inch the walker forward while he or she gingerly ambles forward, using the hemi walker for support. A hemi walker will fold flat for transport in a car. The device is quite stable, but is also quite awkward to use. It requires a lot of practice to get used to. When I finally did get comfortable with it, it gave me a sense of getting better at regaining my mobility. At first, I was allowed to use the hemi walker to assist me in getting out of bed and for supporting me when getting into and out of the wheelchair.

Much like using a cane, the hemi walker is held with the hand opposite the bad leg. In my case, I supported my weight with my left hand. This took much of the weight off my right leg. When taking a step, I would move forward by moving and placing my right foot and the hemi walker in unison. I would support my weight simultaneously with my right leg and left arm. Then I would move my left leg forward and repeat the process. This required a fair amount of coordination and practice before I was able to successfully take more than a few steps at a time.

The first few days of physical therapy were heavily focused on learning to use the hemi walker. I used it to slide out of bed and to turn and get into the wheelchair. Much of this effort came when I was away from the therapy sessions. When in the room, anytime I had to go to the bathroom, it was necessary to use the hemi walker in conjunction with the wheelchair. To use the bathroom, it was necessary to call the nurse's station with the call button. When the nurse would arrive, I had to get into the wheelchair and be wheeled to the bathroom. Then I would be helped back out of the chair and positioned at the commode. The nurse would leave the room and I could go.

Bathroom 101

When I was done doing my business, I would stand up and pull my pants back up, call the nurse, and turn around to get into the wheel chair. Then I would get wheeled back to my bed. I would get out of the chair and, with the hemi walker, I would back up to the bed and then sit back onto it. This was quite a process; it took about ten minutes and required two people to do what I used to do alone in about a minute. Quite frankly, when the nurses were busy or during the night, I had more than a few "accidents" while waiting for the nursing staff. This was expected, though, and the hospital staff was used to it, even if I wasn't.

The aim of my physical therapy at this point was directed toward improving my ability with the hemi walker. We continued to concentrate on getting into and out of the wheelchair, locking (and unlocking) the wheels, moving the footrests out of the way, and twisting the armrest out of the way. It also involved taking a few steps and learning to turn around and come back to the chair, and again turning around and getting back into it.

In the same sessions, I was taken to a large table, where I lay on my back and raised my legs and then bent my knees, starting out at five repetitions and then eventually working my way up to ten reps. This increase in repetitions was very encouraging to me. That's because, in the two weeks since the onset of the stroke, I had lost almost all strength and control in my right leg and, believe it or not, even a lot of the strength in my left leg.

We also went out into the hall more and increased the distance I covered moving myself in the wheelchair. Over time the distance covered went from ten feet to more than fifty feet and back. I got used to knowing where the "mountain ranges" were in the section of the hallway we used. As time went on, we moved to different hallways with more pedestrian traffic and items big and small lining the sides—our very own obstacle course, which, of course, required me to move around things. These "obstacles" included beds that were unused, various IV stands, monitors, and computer work stations. This was much more difficult to maneuver in. Not only was it difficult to maneuver around the pedestrian traffic, but I was constantly turning my head around to see where I was going as well. The worst part, though, was that this new hallway had a new set of mountain ranges to conquer.

Therapy Is Progressing

My physical therapy progressed to relearning to walk, now, however, with the hemi walker. There were three other major rehab apparatuses in the gym. One of these represented a straight stairway. I would walk up four steps to reach a landing and then down four steps on the other side of the apparatus. There were hand railings on both sides, so no need or room there for the hemi walker. This was rough at first. The first thing was that I just plain didn't have the movement available in my right leg to pick it up. After a few days I got used to going up the steps with my left foot first and down the steps with my left leg first.

By using this left-leg-first technique, I was able to use the leg with the maximum strength to maneuver the weight of my body and ease the load on my right leg. Of course, steps were taken one at a time instead of alternating two at a time. Besides my not being able to negotiate steps in the normal manner, it took me about five times as long to go up and down the steps as it would have when I was fully able-bodied. After two and a half years, I still hadn't gotten the hang of going up and down stairs with only one rail, but that could have been for one or two reasons. First, it might have been self-preservation, or it might have been some other sort of mental block. Whatever it was, I have never looked forward to falling and getting hurt. At the time I was writing this, I had rationalized that having one thing I couldn't do (climb and descend stairs) was OK, considering all that I could now proudly do. Well, that was almost four years ago, and now that I'm well into my sixth year poststroke, I can now proclaim that I can easily walk up and down stairways as long as railings are on both sides of the actual steps. I have gone down stairways with a smooth wall to my unaffected side for support, but I do not do this often.

One Small Step for (This) Man

OK, let's go back to my time in the rehab place at the second hospital. The second apparatus for my physical therapy, after the mini-stairway, had a ramp on one end, followed by two steps up to a platform, two other steps down on the side, followed by another step with an angled "riser." The ramp end represented a wheelchair ramp normally found in handicapped parking places. Walking up this ramp at first caused the sensation of losing my equilibrium and, hence, my balance. After a few days of trying to walk up this ramp, my sense of equilibrium was restored and gave me no problem.

The steps on the same side of the ramp I had just gone up had wider "tread," or flat surfaces. On the wider treads, I figured it might be necessary to take a short step to better position myself to make the next step up. When I reached the platform at the top, I found it necessary to make a ninety-degree turn to go down the other steps. These treads are standard tread widths.

The final step represented a curb that is formed at an angle. This required me to move the foot out farther to reach the ground. Unlike the first stairway apparatus, this one had no handrails. All the movement on this apparatus was accomplished with the use of the hemi walker. Because the apparatus required a certain amount of flexibility with the hemi walker, it was the last piece of equipment in the chain of events for inpatient rehab.

The third and final apparatus was a device that simulated getting into and out of a passenger car. It required that I walk up to the door with the hemi walker. My mission was to reach the door and open it without bumping it into myself. Next, I was to again grab the hemi walker and move forward into the opening, turning so that my posterior was aligned with the seat, and then I sat down. The next step was to turn my legs into the seated position, fold the hemi walker, place it to my left side, and close the door. Using my left arm to close a door that was on my right became an adventure, but in time it became manageable. To get out,

I had to reach over to open the door with my left hand, swing my body and feet to the right, unfold the hemi walker and position it, slide outward as far as I could while keeping my posterior on the seat, lean forward to get to an upright position, and walk away. Oh, yeah, don't forget to close the door! Getting into a car is another experience that takes a lot of practice, but once relearned, it can be relatively easy. This apparatus didn't have pedals or a steering wheel, so I guess the unspoken message screaming at me was that I wouldn't be driving again soon.

During physical therapy, I also continued spending time on the bed moving my left leg up to exercise and loosen it. I also performed repetitions of knee bends, and did further exercise by turning my leg to each side as well as pivoting. I also worked on flexing my foot and ankle. At first I would move both feet simultaneously to teach my brain what to do, but ultimately could pretty much work my right leg independently from my left. I also progressed to walking longer distances in the hallway with the hemi walker. A couple of times I was successful when I tried walking without the hemi walker by stepping sideways while holding the railing along the wall with my left hand.

Getting My Brain Involved

Then there was occupational therapy. It involved trying to use my brain to move and control my right arm and hand. This type of activity proved to be the most difficult, and even now (present day) I know it might never recover as well as my right leg has. I talk of controlling my right arm and hand, but in reality the stroke damage involved my right-shoulder movement as well.

Shoulder therapy consisted of moving my right shoulder in conjunction with my left shoulder and ultimately independent from my left shoulder. These movements include moving my shoulder up and down and forward and backward to match the movement of my left shoulder. When inpatient therapy was completed, the range of motion in my right shoulder was about 50 percent of what it was in my left. This motion was independent of my ability to raise my arm at my shoulder, even though you use shoulder muscles to move your upper arm fore and aft, and outward and upward.

Therapy for my elbow was similar to attempting to move my right and left elbows in conjunction with each other. The elbow is a great thing. It allows your hand to move through an arc of approximately two hundred seventy degrees from facing upwardly flat open to open to your outside. My therapy was designed to get as much of that movement back as possible. In addition to rotating your hand, your elbow raises and lowers your arm from being straight, or fully extended, to being bent to within approximately "vee" shape thirty degrees of being closed, or folded flat on itself.

Raise Your Right Arm and . . . Keep Trying

I can now raise my right arm to within the thirty-degree,

closed "vee" shape. Now, before you think I can fully bend it, which would be good, you have to picture this: when standing, the normal position for the arm is straight down at your side. In my case, my new normal position is bent at about a ninety-degree angle across my stomach.

Therapy for my elbow consisted of trying to get the full range of motion to return. At the beginning of therapy, it was difficult to bend my elbow or twist it at all. By continuing to move it, though, I was ultimately able to bend it through about half of the normal range and twist my wrist slightly, from a hand position where my palm is flat on a table position.

Wrist motion is an area where you normally move it in conjunction with your forearm. However, it is sometimes necessary to move it independently, like when swinging a golf club or eating with a fork or spoon. I had about 25 percent range of motion left in my wrist at the beginning of therapy. By continuing to move my wrist, I was able to regain some of its range of motion. This motion is independent of my forearm and is the up-and-down motion as well as side-to-side motion.

This brings me to finger and thumb therapy, the last two individual areas of occupational therapy left to discuss. Finger and thumb therapy consisted of manual stimulation, electrical stimulation, and, eventually, a brace to hold my fingers straight. Manual stimulation of my fingers involved my bending them straight, one at a time, and then all four at a time. I would move them in my room as well as in the gym. While I couldn't control the movement of my fingers, I could at least prevent them from becoming atrophied or frozen in place by manually bending and straightening them with my left hand.

One Saturday afternoon, my occupational therapist was working with her other patients. Even though I wasn't scheduled to see her, she came to my room and said she had an hour to kill and wanted to try something if I were game. Of course!

"E-Stemming"

We went to another gym on another floor of the hospital, where she got out an E-stem device, as she started to explain it to me. "E-stem" was short for electrical stimulation, and immediately I was interested. She proceeded to place two stimulator contacts to my forearm in different places. She then set the electrical-current levels and duration of stimulation to apply electrical stimulation to the nerve structures in my arm to move the muscles that moved my fingers. Normally, the stimulation was set to rest for about twenty seconds and then apply current for about ten seconds. I had her set the stimulation quite high, probably higher than she really wanted to, but I was determined to see what it could do.

This stimulation lifted only one finger at a time. It also caused me to lift my wrist if the contacts were placed in the right places. While it might not seem like much, just seeing my fingers and wrist move was truly an amazing thing. After each finger was stimulated a few times, she would reposition the contacts and another finger would be stimulated. I would feel a few seconds of electrical current and then watch my fingers actually move!

In addition to trying to regain individual arm muscle movement, the therapist had me work on multiple muscle movements. One device she used was like a skateboard, although smaller—about eight inches long and five inches wide, with swivel casters instead of fixed-direction wheels. The idea behind using this device was to get my elbow to move sideways as well as my shoulder to move forward and rearward. It felt very bulky to move, and I had very little success with it after using it a few times.

During subsequent sessions, my therapist would try to create the same movement using a dry wash cloth on a table top. She would clean the table top off to make sure there was little resistance to movement due to any smudges, dirt, or similar obstructions on the surface. Then she would place a wash cloth on the surface. I would move my hand onto the wash cloth and move it through as much of an arc as I could. While the movement was not much, I was able to get some movement of the wash cloth on the table.

The final thing she did was form a brace that would hold my wrist in an extended fashion with my fingers out. My first finger joint from the knuckle was held straight in the brace, but the second and third joints were allowed to be bent with it. The purpose of this brace was to try to straighten the wrist and fingers in a more natural state and get my brain to remember this position. I wore this brace with very minor success for two or three times a day for a period of an hour or so at a time.

Chapter 3

Life in
the Hospital

THERAPY WAS GREAT, BUT THERE WERE STILL ABOUT TWENTY-ONE OTHER HOURS LEFT IN THE DAY. It's not dead time or down time, though; there's still plenty of work to be done, mostly by the patient. That remaining time each day is as important to recovery as is the therapy. There is much more that can be done in the hospital room.

After the first week in that second hospital, the staff moved me off the third floor and into a room at the end of one wing of the second floor. The third-floor rehab section was filling up with patients, and they needed the space for those who were in worse shape than I was and required more attention. My new room was much larger and had far more guest seating available. It was also much quieter on the second floor, thanks to the lower occupancy. The scenery out the window was much nicer as well.

In addition to having chairs for about eight visitors, my new room had enough open space to allow me to move around in the wheelchair some as time progressed and I made small, incremental improvements in what I could do. In addition, the room had a decent recliner next to the bed.

Most of the therapy was completed in the morning, so I would spend a few hours a day in the recliner in the afternoons. I could sit up in it and surf the Internet with my laptop, or I could recline the chair back and read, or even take short naps in it. Unfortunately, any time I wanted to move from the bed, or from the wheelchair, or from the recliner, I needed assistance, although I would have preferred to not need the help. Deep down, I knew it was a good idea to have the assistance, and there also was a certain amount of potential liability on the hospital's part, so I never seriously challenged any of the staff. It still felt funny, however, hitting the call button and waiting for a staff member to come help me whenever I wanted to move.

A Visit from the Psychologist

After being in this other hospital for about a week, I was visited by the staff psychologist. He was there to see if he could offer me something in the way of encouragement. His questions and comments were quite timely, but I had already reached the conclusions he was leading me to. I told him that it was my time for a break, or vacation, even if it was a major life-changing event. Instead of concentrating my efforts on selling my next car, I had to concentrate on my steps to recovery, taking them one step at a time and staying positive. That was welcome news to the psychologist, and he left me alone the rest of the time I was there.

Away from the therapy sessions, I was able to eventually move around the room a bit more, both with and without the wheelchair. This primarily involved getting up and using the bathroom, but even that seemed like a major victory. My walking still consisted of taking steps eight inches at a time. To put that into perspective, the normal distance for a step for most people is between twenty and thirty inches. Still, being able to use the hemi walker to use the bathroom was by far much easier than using the wheelchair. Getting to the bathroom on my own took a few weeks to accomplish, and it was still "supervised" by a nurse; I had to press the call button and wait for the nurse to come to the room before I could get out of bed.

Speaking of the call button, even though it was (for the most part) a good friend, at times it was a bit inconvenient. The bed had a sensor in it that would go off when my weight was not over it. At least once every two days, I would roll over on the bed without putting any weight on the sensor. I hated it for the nurses who had to come in for the "false alarm." There were also times that the button would fall off the bed. These times were interesting, as it was hard to get it back up onto the bed with my having only one arm that worked. I really felt bad putting the nurses through the extra work, but they were always gracious about it.

Bathroom 201

While I was eventually able to use the hemi walker to go to and from the bathroom, I would always use the wheelchair to get to the shower, brush my teeth, and shave. Showering required a shower seat. In order to use the shower seat, I would disrobe, slide out of the wheelchair, and sit on the shower seat, close the curtain, and slide into the shower. When taking a shower, I learned to use the hand-held shower head and, obviously, only my left hand to apply soap, shampoo, and to rinse the soap and shampoo off. I would let the shower head lie beside me on the seat while I soaped up, then pick it up with my left hand and rinse the soap off. I used the same technique for my hair. While somewhat inconvenient compared to what I was used to (using two hands), I was able to shower and always felt invigorated afterward. The nurses would always be in the room with me, which was reassuring.

The worst part about showering was being awakened at 5:00 A.M. by the nurse and being asked if I was ready for my shower. My response was typically something along the lines of it being the middle of the night, and I am on vacation for goodness sake. The night nurse was on duty until seven in the morning and was usually bored. He was looking for something to do, I guess.

Brushing my teeth was interesting in the wheelchair. The sinks in the room were open underneath to allow the wheelchair to get close to the edge of the sink, but it was not close enough to allow me to bend over the sink far enough to rinse out my mouth after I was done brushing my teeth. I would end up with at least some water on the edge of the sink and would have to clean up the mess. I guess that was part of the way I was raised—to not leave any place a mess.

Shaving was a similar process to brushing my teeth. I hadn't shaved with an electric razor since I was twenty-one. Shaving with my left hand was a new experience to me. I just plain didn't have the ability at first to shave as closely as I usually had. I hadn't shaved for the first couple of weeks that I was in the hospital. Unfortunately, my beard had quite a bit of gray in spots, and it also was itchy, so I decided to shave it one morning. It took me quite a while, first due to the length of the beard, and, secondly, it was the first time I had used my left hand to shave. It was a challenge at first because I had never done it. I was accustomed to using my right hand and maneuvering the razor to the various contours of my face, chin, and neck. At first, I was terrible at shaving left-handed. I was just not doing a good job holding the blade against my skin. At one time I actually watched myself trying to use the end of the blade, or ninety degrees to the cutting surface, which in no way even has the metal blades. When I got used to using my left hand, it became as much second nature as using my right hand. One thing about shaving— it was worth it in the end, as I felt civil again.

I had the luxury of being able to go to a table in the nurses' station pretty much any time I wanted to. Unfortunately, I really found this a tad uneventful. Most of the time I would be the only patient there, and the nurses were so busy that there was little or no social interaction. If there were any other patients there, they were usually in pretty tough shape and were difficult to communicate with. By the end of my first week in the hospital I was no longer sitting there. The opportunity was well-intentioned, but it had actually become too boring. I could make better use of my time back in my room reading or checking out things on the Internet.

Journaling

In addition to spending time in my room online with Facebook and checking my email, I started a daily journal of my activities. This was more than a bit time-consuming with only the use of my left hand. I never was a fast typist, but it took a *lot* longer with one hand. I thought that the journal idea would be great to mark my improvements and keep a record of achieving major milestones. However, I quit making entries after a few weeks. My improvements were coming fewer and farther in between, and the journal lost its emphasis for me. On top of all that, my laptop would eventually be hit by a virus a few months later, and I lost all the files on it, including a month's worth of data in my poststroke journal. As a result, everything in this book is totally from memory. I have done my best to remember the highlights of my stroke events, and I feel that the things not covered would be beyond the scope and purpose of this book anyway.

I spent a lot of time reading books and magazines, as well as watching television. I had been really too busy before the stroke to do as much reading as I would have liked to, so this allowed me more opportunity with this activity. While my reading time was welcome, I also spent time watching TV, in particular the History Channel. I have very few regular TV shows that I "have to" watch, but I do like to watch TV shows from which I can learn something.

I became somewhat addicted to *American Pickers* and *Pawn Stars*. At the time, Mike Wolf was opening his second Antique Archeology store in the old Marathon Motors building in Nashville, so this was exciting to me—meaningful because of its proximity to where I live. Surprisingly, he eventually married a woman from Leiper's Fork, Tennessee, a small town south of Nashville. This made him practically native to many of us in Tennessee. *Pawn Stars* was better entertainment, but it was neat to see the history of most of their items.

Atlas Shrugged (for a Third Time)

In addition to using the laptop and TV for things to do, I had Tami bring my book *Atlas Shrugged* for me to read. I had started reading it for the third time a week before having the stroke. Author Ayn Rand wrote this book in 1957, writing it in a style somewhat different to what you might read today from current authors. At about one thousand fifty pages long, it also was the longest novel written in its day. By reading a few pages at a time, it would take some time to read. I figured I had the time available in the hospital to make a lot of headway, and I actually finished it in two weeks. A good friend stopped by for a visit one afternoon and brought me some magazines, which occupied my reading time for my remaining days in the hospital. By keeping my mind engaged, all this reading really helped me some with my overall recovery.

About two and a half weeks into my stay in this hospital, another doctor paid me a visit. He asked me a bunch of questions about my diet and how much I had been eating and drinking. An analysis of my blood had shown that I was getting dehydrated, and he wanted to build up my levels before it became a problem. Some adjustments were made to my diet, including drinking more fluids and taking another pill daily. The menu changed slightly with a few more choices, and I started to eat somewhat more from it, and I drank more. A few days later, the doctor who had queried me about my diet came back and said I had improved. He was happy, but I kept taking the added medication until I left the hospital.

Four days before I was to go home, when the dietician came to my room to fill out the menu for the next day. I jokingly asked her if I could have a bacon cheeseburger and French fries the next day. I hadn't had a burger for nearly four weeks and wanted one more than anything in the world. Imagine my excitement the next day, a bacon cheeseburger and fries showed up for my dinner. Of course, it was hospital room quality (which is quite a few steps below hospital cafeteria quality), but to me it was like having a steak.

When I suffered the stroke, my weight had been about one hundred seventy-five pounds. I had done enough physical work to stay in good shape and maintain a really low body mass index (BMI) number. In fact, my BMI was low enough that most men half my age would have been envious. During my time in the hospital, my weight dropped to less than a hundred fifty pounds. This was a good thing, even though I had lost my ability to perform most of the physical stuff I had done before the stroke.

Prior to my hospitalization, I had never taken any prescriptions for more than about a week or two at a time. That was a record I was very proud of, although it came to an end once I had the stroke. It seems I was taking pills or getting shots for everything. I was given pills for cholesterol, blood pressure, blood thinners, insulin shots for diabetes, and Lord knows what else. And then there was the dehydration, and for a couple of nights even sleeping pills. This was a whole new phase in my life, and I wasn't sure what to make of it. I had crossed a threshold I had never imagined I would have to face.

Medications

One afternoon my brother called and I explained to him all the medications that I was taking. He told me that for years he had been taking as many medications as I was now getting, although his weren't necessarily the same medications I was being given. Finally, he told me that his wife was taking as many as sixty-five pills a day. Six years earlier, she had had a heart and lung transplant, and she had been on these medications to stabilize the transplants.

That conversation with my brother immediately yielded several insights. First, the medications I was taking in the hospital had no adverse effects on me, other than that original blood pressure reduction medication (Hydralazine HCl) in the ER. I had known so many people who had become dependent on drugs that I had determined I never wanted to be in that group. I was very fortunate that during my stroke recovery I was never in any pain, so I never had taken any pain killers, such as those addictive opioids. I never had any potential addictions as a result. Over time, I have come off most medications and don't feel any negative effects from any of the medications I have taken.

Another conclusion I reached was that if my family members were taking medication that helped them even in a small way, I should consider the use of some medications to be acceptable. In addition to my conversation with my brother, subsequent conversations with friends indicated a lot of them were taking various medications and felt comfortable doing so.

Finally, when I learned how many medications my sister-in-law was taking, I could not complain about my taking a few pills a day. Obviously, I had some major changes coming up in my life; however, knowing what my sister-in-law had gone through made my problems seem insignificant. She was originally given a chance to live another five years with her transplant surgery, and in fact she has lived another eleven years so far. No matter how unfortunate I was, there is always someone in worse shape than I am. This theme has been brought out ever since, revealing itself to me at least once a month, if not more.

While in the hospital, I had a lot of company. Quite a few former neighbors visited me, as did a number of people from work, as well as a number of other friends. What *really* mattered was that Tami made it her number-one goal to visit me every day. She would have Emma, my granddaughter, and her fiancé, Mike, with her most of the time, as well as Mike's daughter, Mikayla, on weekends. Tami brought a lot of my clothes so I wouldn't have to wear hospital gowns, and she periodically took clothing home and laundered it.

After a few weeks, I could tell that Tami was getting exhausted from coming to the hospital every day. So I told her to take a night off once in a while, starting the next night. I had to tell her that I was a big boy and that if anything happened to me, I really could not be safer than in the hospital. The next night she did not come, and she looked much better the next time she came in. She did call me every day, however. I made sure she took a couple of other nights off before I was discharged.

Every time Emma came with Tami, she brought me some "artwork." Mikayla also brought some of hers in on the days when she came in. That was really sweet, and we posted them to the walls in my room. One day, Emma brought a card signed by everyone in her second-grade class. That was truly special to me. Mike's mother came to visit several times, and she would always bring someone with her. On Christmas Day, half of her family came to spend almost an hour after their dinner was done. That was a pretty nice thing to do; that, along with some other friends stopping by earlier in the day, made it a Christmas to remember for sure.

Midway through my last week in the hospital, I was visited by a representative from a medical equipment company. He was there to arrange for the equipment I would need after my discharge from the "five-star hotel" in which I had been spending my vacation time. I needed three things: my own hemi walker, a shower seat, and what would be my very own custom-fit wheelchair. The hemi walker had adjustable legs, so it did not require anything other than to be adjusted for my height. The shower seat was pretty much the same, but it was adjusted to fit the bathtub at my daughter's house. Each bathtub is slightly different relative to its bottom, the floor, and the height of the front tub wall. The final adjustments would have to wait.

The wheelchair was a different story. The seat height had to be set so that my knees would allow my lower legs and feet to touch the ground. The side rails had to be the right height for my arms to rest on them. In addition, there was a swing-out shelf on the right armrest for my right arm to rest on. This was to prevent my arm from dropping into the wheel. Finally, the footrests had to be adjusted to keep my feet off the ground when someone was pushing me. All of these measurements were taken, and the wheelchair, hemi walker, and shower seat were delivered on the Friday morning when I was to be discharged.

Thursday was my last day of physical and occupational therapy at the hospital. The therapists gave me last-minute instructions. I was then given my waist belt to be used for walking with the hemi walker, the brace that was made to keep my fingers and wrist straight, two pairs of walking socks, and a few other things. When Tami visited that Thursday night, we started taking the artwork off the walls and started packing to get ready to go Friday. I almost hated to see that phase end.

Time to Check Out

Friday morning finally came and I was pretty excited to finally check out of the "five-star" hospital. After I got ready for the day, a steady chain of visitors stopped in to visit. The doctor in charge of my therapy was among the first to visit. We discussed future outpatient therapy, and she said that the hospital staff would be coming by with more details. She was happy with my recovery and encouraged me to continue just as I had been doing. We also set an appointment to meet in three months.

The staff psychologist stopped in to make sure my attitude was OK and to answer any questions I had. He offered to see me at any time if I thought I could use his help, but I never called him. I really liked him, but I was not going to waste his time when others could better use him.

The nursing supervisor came in and reviewed medications that had been prescribed for me going forward. These had also been discussed with my own personal doctor and my neurologist. Appointments had been made with them as well. She had asked what pharmacy I was going to use and made arrangements with them to pick up the medications at a local pharmacy.

A hospital business office representative came up to my room to get my contact information She said she would be back with the finished release information, as well as outpatient therapy arrangements with another affiliated hospital near Tami's home.

Finally, the lady from the medical equipment company came in. She had a brand new wheelchair, a hemi walker, and shower seat for me. I had to pay for the shower seat and hemi walker, but the wheelchair was under a lease agreement through my insurance company. After the financial arrangements were settled, we made the final adjustments to the wheelchair and hemi walker, and then she left. The large room was rapidly getting filled up with the equipment I needed at home.

Tami and Mike came up in the early afternoon, and we finished packing and then waited for the office representative to return. She came by in mid-afternoon. After going over the final paperwork, I was finally released. After we loaded up Tami's car with my stuff, we drove away from the hospital. It was nice to be on the outside again, but I was still just a bit apprehensive about what was in store for the next few months. Nevertheless, *freedom*!!!!

For nearly seven years after my stroke, I have had a lot of ups and downs. All of the "downs" have been resolved as much as possible over time, leaving me to continue looking forward to an incredibly bright future. Now, don't get me wrong when I say an incredibly bright future. Most people would probably look at my stroke "condition" as a real bummer and not live up to their new potential, but it is possible to still have a bright future if you allow yourself to. I am never going to run the Music City Marathon with my daughter Tami, never again going to turn a lap at Nashville Superspeedway at over 140 mph, but I can walk without a cane again, and I am working very hard at not dragging my affected foot.

Chapter 4

Moving in with My Daughter

AFTER LEAVING THE HOSPITAL CAMPUS, WE MADE A COU-
PLE OF STOPS ON THE WAY TO TAMI'S HOUSE. She and
Mike had obtained a nice, gently used queen-sized bed
for me to sleep in while I stayed there. It would end up
being a very comfortable bed for me.

My granddaughter and Mike's daughter slept in the
second bedroom on bunk beds, which left Tami the third
bedroom free for her to use as a home office and catchall
room. That was eventually going to become my room.
Mike had found time to assemble the bed frame and put
the box spring and mattress on it, but because of visiting
me in the hospital so much, they had not had the time to
get sheets and pillows. So we stopped at a department
store and bought sheets and a mattress pad. At the same
time, Tami bought me two new golf shirts. The next stop

we made was to get a handicapped shower head as well as an inexpensive shower curtain. We made these purchases right next to the department store, so moving from one to the other was fairly easy.

Being in a wheelchair was not something totally new, but being in the wheelchair outside the hospital was a little bit scary as well as frustrating. We didn't have a handicap placard yet for the car, so I would get unloaded at the store curbs and would sit there with Mike and the kids while Tami parked the car.

Going Shopping

The department store was one of my favorite stores. I had shopped there for years buying clothes, shoes, some home decor, small appliances, and the like. One thing I had never paid attention to was how narrow the aisles were. The main aisles were wide enough to get between departments, but the side aisles were quite narrow. They were narrow enough that if the merchandise was positioned forward enough from the shelves, a person in a wheelchair was going to rub against it passing by.

We went in the bedding department, and I helped pick out sheets and pillows. Tami and Mike wanted to look at other options, so they left me in one of the aisles while they walked off. After a couple minutes, I started to feel abandoned, so I decided to use the "push backward with one foot" trick to go find them. I located them two aisles away, which was less than twenty feet, but I was glad to have found them, and I felt pretty good about my in-store maneuverability, as limited as it was.

Tami decided what to purchase, and we got the bedding. My lap became the shopping cart, and we headed for the front of the store.

The "Big Box" store was pretty nicely arranged with plenty of space in the aisles to get the wheelchair through. Mike and I picked out the shower head, while Tami went for the shower curtain, and she took the shopping cart with her. Once again, my lap became the depository for "stuff." I wasn't too sure how I felt about my lap being used as a shopping cart, but then again I used that as an incentive to improve my walking as quickly as possible.

When we finally got home from shopping, it was time to get everything organized—all my stuff from the hospital as well as what we had just purchased. Tami, Mike, and Emma hauled my suitcase, the bags of things from the hospital, and the bags from our shopping excursion into the house. I took charge of getting myself from the car into the house. It took as long for me to get into the house as it did to get the rest of everything else in. In the end, my trip into the house was a success, reminiscent of the first time I had walked on that off-level concrete at the hospital. I made it up the four steps to the porch, entered the house with a storm door and step, and got my coat off. That was a major accomplishment, and I was grateful for being among family and out of the hospital. I even was sitting in one of Tami's dining room chairs, another first, in a month's time. For some reason, that felt really good to be sitting at that table stacked full of stuff from the day.

Tami got to work making the bed with the new sheets, as well as creating some room in the closet for my clothes. That took a while as she moved some of her clothes into her own closet and packed quite a few things that were in her closet into storage containers and moved them into the garage. Mike got busy calling his brother Chris to arrange for him to make railings for the front porch steps. He sent pictures of the steps with measurements. After that was done, he got busy and put the handicapped shower head in the guest bathroom. We put the shower seat in place, and cut the shower curtain to work as well. It was beginning to feel like home for me.

When I finally got to bed, I felt like I was sleeping in luxury compared to the hospital bed. I had a whole queen-sized bed to myself, with new sheets, pillows, and a nice comforter. I snuggled in for a good night of sleep. I have always slept lying on my stomach, with both of my arms under the pillow. I was always asleep within about five minutes, and very seldom woke up until the next morning. While in the hospital, I learned that I could not sleep like this any longer due to the lack of movement in my right side. I never had a good night's sleep in the hospital, but this new bed was comfortable, and the first night I slept well, even though I would still wake up several times during the night.

Saturday morning was New Year's Eve. After I got ready for the day, Mike had a few more measurements to take as well as a few more pictures to take for his brother to use in making alterations in and around the house. Mike's brother called back soon after with a list of materials that we needed to get, and he said he would be over around noon with a friend to put the railings up. We went over to Lowe's and got the materials. That was my first time in a Lowe's store in a wheelchair, and it was somewhat difficult emotionally. For one thing, I felt self-conscious. What made it emotionally hard was that I had been to Lowe's nearly once or more nearly every week before I had the stroke, and always had walked. I did, however, feel good about being there in another way, as I was once again going to be involved in a building project, even on a limited basis. We returned home with the materials by about 11 A.M.

Chris and his friend showed up about 11:30 and started working on the railings. Chris is the supervisor for a roofing company and runs several roofing crews on a regular basis. His buddy was a finish carpenter for a new construction company. They did an absolutely fantastic job putting up very sturdy and attractive railings. I went outside and watched the work being done, mostly from the swing on the porch, but I also got down the steps and watched from the ground as well. I did more walking and standing using the hemi walker that afternoon than I had done in the whole month in the hospital. Emotionally it was a rough time, because it was the first construction project, however small or large, on a home project that I had to just watch without being involved with my own hands. It was a very interesting New Year's Eve.

On New Year's Day, Tami, Mike, and I went back to my apartment. I had a list of things in mind that I would need to have in order to live at Tami's house for a long-term recovery period; the sooner we got my things moved, the better off I would be. All I had for the room in Tami's house was a comfortable bed and a small desk. What we moved from my apartment included my desktop computer, my nightstand and lamp, my dresser, my twenty-inch TV, various bills and other paperwork, a few books to re-read, and quite a few more clothes and toiletries for me.

While Mike loaded up Tami's CUV (crossover utility vehicle), she and I made sure we had the refrigerator and pantry empty, and then we closed up the apartment. The last step was to turn the heat as low as it could go. I longingly looked at my Suburban and Mustang as we left, knowing it would be a while before I would see them again, let alone drive them, and off we went to my new home for the next few months.

When we arrived at Tami's house, she and Mike moved all of my things inside. Mike hooked up my desktop computer with a set of surplus speakers he had, then brought my dresser, nightstand, and TV into the room, while Tami made even more room in the closet and hung up my clothes. That night I felt much better having most of my essentials and a few luxuries with me.

Bills and Social Security

After the holidays were over, and Tami and Mike had gone back to work, it was time for me to concentrate on several projects. I had to first figure out my finances. During the past month, Tami had been paying my minimum bills for me out of her own pocket, and I was very thankful, but they were my bills and it was my responsibility to pay them going forward. I had to find out from my employer what was necessary to maintain my health insurance. I had to determine when my outpatient therapy was going to start and what it was going to actually consist of. I had to contact Social Security and find out what benefits I could qualify for and how to become enrolled in their programs. I had to review what doctor appointments were upcoming, go over doctor and hospital bills, and develop plans to pay them. There were minor things like a handicapped parking placard, getting power of attorney for Tami, and other things to take care of as well.

I logged onto the Social Security website the first day Tami and Mike went back to work. I made an appointment at the local office, but it was several weeks away, and for several days I received no confirmation message. I had never waited three weeks for information about anything, either in my business or personal life. I talked to Tami about this that night when she arrived home from work. We decided that she would take a day off later in the week and go to the Social Security office, as well as to the county clerk's to get a handicapped parking placard.

The Social Security office for the county that Tami lives in was located in an older professional building in the north side of the county. We brought the wheelchair, just in case, and that was a good move. Maneuvering through the parking lot and up to the front door with the hemi walker would have been extremely difficult. The parking lot was anything but flat, and we had to park quite some distance from the door. Upon entering the building, we found ourselves in a fairly small waiting room. There was seating for about sixty people, and all but one seat in the middle were occupied. A uniformed, armed guard was positioned at the rear of the room along a wall. The armed guard made me wonder just what kind of a situation I was getting involved in.

After what seemed like a short forty-five minutes, we were ushered into the office, where we met with a Social Security case worker. After explaining my situation, the case worker printed what seemed like twenty-five pages that showed my life's work history, starting with my first job at age sixteen. It seemed like a great meeting and answered quite a few questions. This was a large part of my new life, which is why I discuss my finances in Chapter 8.

The trip to the county clerk's office was uneventful. The parking lot was empty, so I decided to walk in with Tami and using the hemi walker. We walked up to the window, told the lady why we were there, and a few minutes later walked out with a bright blue handicapped placard. I guess it was pretty obvious to her why it was needed. The stop was the first time I used the hemi walker to walk into a public place. It physically wore me out, but it was worth the effort in giving me another lesson in what I was capable of, and getting the placard was another tool to make my life easier.

Tami and I took two other steps early on in the stroke-recovery period that may or may not have been necessary, but they made sense at the time. The first was to obtain a legitimate power of attorney for Tami to handle my affairs. My reasoning was that if anything happened to me that would have prevented me from conducting my own affairs, I wanted her to be able to step in for me. Fortunately, there was never a need for her to perform any of these functions, but we both felt better by having this contingency covered. The other was to visit my bank and have her signature authorized for use on my checking account. There were two reasons for this: one was in case anything happened to me; the other was I had obviously lost my ability to write with my right hand, and had not yet developed proficient writing ability with my left hand.

Tami filled out a change-of-address form on my behalf so that all of my mail would come to her house instead of my apartment. In some small way that made me think I was giving in to permanently living the rest of my life with my daughter. Rather than let the thought of permanence get me down, I just used the thought as another incentive to move back to my home as soon as I was able. It's really funny how little things, such as having a positive attitude, can help in the long run.

I called my employer's human resources woman to check on the status of my health insurance coverage. She told me that I was still covered under the regular policy, but would have to continue paying my monthly co-pay of approximately $85 a month. She would keep me on a medical leave of absence as long as she could. The co-pay was due in the middle of the month, and I could mail it in as we went forward. We made a trip one afternoon to my employer to pay the insurance for the first month and pick up my personal items. I had a couple of confidential files on my computer that I used to track my performance, training, and goals. I printed these off and sent them to my personal computer at home before deleting them.

Most of my personal items had been put in a box, but some had not. I was in my wheelchair at the time, so my supervisor searched for the remaining items. I had two screwdrivers, a pair of channel lock pliers, and a really nice umbrella that I could not locate right away. After searching for some time, we found the screwdrivers and pliers in another salesperson's desk, but the umbrella was nowhere to be found. That was my favorite umbrella that I had obtained during a golf outing with a former employer. I hated to lose it, but realistically could not hold it and walk with the hemi walker or a cane anyway. I was a bit taken aback that most of the people I had worked with for a couple of years did not seem to care if I was there or not and that my M&M's and potato chips had gone missing, but I didn't want them anyway. Overall, I was happy that the insurance was continuing.

As for that spreadsheet on my computer which I use to track my personal budget, I still use it even though it is so old; it is very efficient, easy to use, and relevant. I updated this with the information from Tami as to what she had spent, both from her own funds and out of my checking account. I discontinued my telephone landline service at the apartment. I had only used it for fax transmissions anymore, and really no longer needed it with the ultimate closure of my cleaning company. I also discontinued my TV cable service at the apartment. These two services wouldn't be used for several months, and it made no sense to keep paying for them.

I also contacted the leasing agent at my apartment complex, thinking it would make sense to cancel my lease as well. My lease would expire in August, and if I could store my things it would be great to not have to pay rent for space I was not using. The lease could be ended, but I would have to pay the equivalent of three months' rent. Plus, renting an additional storage place would have been about one-third as the cost of rent, so I decided to keep paying rent and see what happened in the coming months.

Here Come More Bills

Doctors' and hospital bills started arriving in the mail as well. I put these in a pile for the time being, because the health insurance had not made any payments on these yet. I got the bills sorted after a few months, dividing them into local providers (those located in the city my apartment was in) and those ones that were not in my city. I then made arrangements to pay off the "local" providers first, because these were the smallest amounts due, and I would have to rely on these providers going forward for most of my long-term care. I discuss my bill-payment plan in greater detail in Chapter 8.

I had scheduled three follow-up appointments with my doctors—my general practitioner, my neurologist, and my therapy doctor. Two of these three were approximately six months off, and one, an appointment with the neurologist, was three months away. I made note of these on a calendar and didn't concern myself with them until the time for the appointments.

I received a phone call from what would be my third hospital regarding the outpatient therapy late in the first week at Tami's house. My insurance company had authorized sixteen sessions each of physical therapy, occupational therapy, and speech therapy. These sessions were each to be an hour long. We would combine them into three hour-long sessions that I could knock out in one trip to the hospital. We scheduled an assessment of my abilities for the following week, at which time the three therapists would each plan a best course of action for me.

The first week was quite busy with planning, organizing, and getting comfortable in my new environment. By the end of the week, I was pretty excited about what was coming up in the next few months. I was ready to give all that I could to getting my life back in order to the best of my ability.

Chapter 5

Outpatient Therapy

O UTPATIENT THERAPY WAS AT A THIRD HOSPITAL THAT WAS LOCATED NEAR MY DAUGHTER'S HOME. It was typically scheduled for ten in the morning. I was still in the wheelchair when the therapy started, and Tami took me to the hospital. This worked well for two visits, but she could not take off much more time. Fortunately, Mike's mother, Bonnie, was retired and could provide transportation. Her provision of transportation was a Godsend, and I very much appreciate her efforts and the sacrifice of her time.

Speech therapy as an outpatient lasted two sessions. My speech had recovered fairly well; other than speaking softly, I could enunciate my words well. My eating and swallowing were coming along nicely, and there was little that could be done to improve in this area. I could read and pronounce all of the therapist's word lists of three- and four-syllable words and her sentences appropriately. The therapist learned that my speech pattern had always been soft and somewhat rapid, so I was close to speaking normally. She was satisfied that my speech was coherent and that my thoughts appropriately matched my speech. I have since been working to concentrate on slowing my speech a little and on being somewhat louder. Overall, it seems to be a little better than it was even prior to the stroke.

I had two great therapists for occupational therapy and physical therapy. The two of them worked closely together and often crossed into each other's specialties to some extent. When the two therapists "crossed paths," it worked quite well, although when they concentrated on their respective specialties enough, I never forgot who did what. Both types of therapy were really continuations of what I had been doing with inpatient therapists, but these therapists added their own "twists" to the process.

The occupational therapist (OT) started out by having me drag a wash cloth on the tabletop with my right hand, similar to what I had done during inpatient therapy. She modified this to having me reach for objects and try to pick them up. Amazingly, the first objects that she had me try to pick up were tire air fill valves. I was able, with a lot of effort, to move my arm and hand to be able to make contact with the valve, but I was unable to move it. That felt good, but not good enough. At least it showed me that some recovery was possible. She ultimately tried this with other smaller objects with the same results.

Another relatively small thing the OT did early on was modify the brace for keeping my wrist and fingers extended. Since this was a piece of plastic, it was a matter of heating and shaping the plastic, forming it to fit. Her idea was to bend my fingers backward and to relax my thumb somewhat. She also added more straps to hold my wrist flat in relation to my arm. I would use this brace throughout the outpatient therapy as well as for up to two hours while I slept—and this went on for about two years. Later on I would only use it two or three times a week.

Another area in which I "crossed over" was in my use of a wheeled walker with a block mounted on it to hold my wrist at a ninety-degree angle to my arm while I walked without dragging my right foot. Even though we tried this for several visits, the results were less than successful. I would end up being bent over at my waist with the walker leaning way forward and my right foot still dragging. Some people say that the definition of insanity is to keep doing the same thing over and over and expecting different results. After trying this five times before dropping this form of my therapy, we achieved different results, and I eventually walked a distance of twenty feet by the time we stopped. Some progress was being made, but this exercise was way beyond my new abilities.

The remainder of occupational therapy was moving my arm through whatever range of motion I could, with slight increases in these ranges as I continued. This included raising my arm in front of my body and sideways as well. Throughout the therapy, I found it difficult to bend my right elbow. It improved ever so slightly rather than in any significant way. I do remember one night at dinner, sitting next to Mike, and raising my arm across my chest with my elbow bent and pushing against his hand with a fair amount of strength. It was a victory to me to be able to show that I still had the strength, if not the dexterity.

The outpatient gym was a large rectangular room with offices in the middle of the room. Each time I was there, I would walk around the gym. The distance I walked was about one hundred ten feet. At first it was difficult, but by the time I was done with sixteen therapy sessions, I was able to make it that distance fairly comfortably, although I heavily dragged my right foot. During the time in therapy there, I went from being in a wheelchair for basic transportation to using the hemi walker, and ended up walking with a cane. This took about eight weeks of therapy and working on my walking at home.

The physical therapist (PT) also had an adjustable height table/bed available. As was done during my inpatient therapy, we used the table a fair amount. My time on the table was spent primarily on my back moving my right leg into various positions. I would bend it at the hip to the right and left. This usually involved ten repetitions with both legs. It was far easier with my left leg, but I could move my right leg almost as far to the right and left. We would bend my leg up from my hip, first with my knee straight and then bending my knee. We also tried bending my right foot sideways and up and down. Again, this involved repetitions and came easily to me.

One of the things we used a few times off the bed was an elliptical machine. This was easy for me, so we stopped using it as I was not gaining anything from it. The gym was also equipped with a stairway similar to what we had in the first hospital. There was a difference between inpatient and outpatient, though, in that the outpatient steps were much steeper, and there were six steps instead of just three on the inpatient gym's stairway. We mastered these steps as well as could be expected.

Time for Some Reps

To do deep knee bends, we used a railing, usually trying again for ten repetitions. At first I realized that I was primarily using my left leg. It became necessary for me to consciously tell my brain to put forth the effort to primarily use my right leg to perform these deep knee bends. Finally, we used a full-length mirror for me to observe the differences in the actions of my left and right legs. Believe it or not, this helped me quite a bit to see just how the movement varied between my two legs. I would focus on getting the movements in both legs to be similar.

Concentrating on using similar movement between both legs is, surprisingly, very difficult. More than three years after my therapy ended, I still found that this concentration was necessary, especially outdoors while walking longer distances. This also applies to hand and arm movement. In my early stages of occupational therapy, I often would move my left hand to get my right to move at some level. Obviously, my right hand wouldn't move in any way near the extent of my left hand, but it seemed to help the movement in my right hand.

If you will recall, I was told at the time of the stroke that within twelve months a stroke victim would regain 90 percent of the total amount of ultimate recoverable use of affected limbs. I am determined to come closer to a full recovery than that. Nearly every day, I can do more than the day before. These are admittedly *very* small gains, but, no matter, these were gains in my abilities and should be considered positive. My personal goal is to get nearly full use of my right leg and arm back at some point in my lifetime.

My PT was a young woman who was very enthusiastic about advancing her education and improving her abilities. During my therapy, she went out of town to a local two-day seminar and a full week-long seminar. When she would return from these seminars, she would want to try something new. Some of these things worked and some didn't, but, like her, I was ready to try anything at least once. Those that seemed like they had the potential to help were incorporated into my long-term therapy.

Both of my outpatient therapists were very good at using various devices to assist me. In two cases these devices were purchased custom-made for me, but the most

interesting and helpful devices were those that were im-
provised by the two therapists themselves.

Dragging the Line

My PT believed that I could reduce the amount of dragging
of my right foot with a brace to keep my foot-to-calf angle
at ninety degrees. She sent me to a medical device manufacturer located in town. Mike took me there twice. The
first time was to measure my foot and calf, and the second
to make sure the brace fit properly for me to wear it. The
brace was a thin piece of plastic formed and strapped to my
calf to hold the upper part in place. The lower part fit my
foot contour but left my toes free to flex. The lower section
was retained by my shoe. This device helped my foot to
some degree, but it also emphasized that I needed to improve my movement toward my hip and knee to lift my
foot higher during my walking motion. This movement
took me almost three years to improve, and it is not second
nature. It requires concentration to walk and keep from
dragging my foot. If I lose my concentration it will cause
me to drag my foot slightly. Still, it is much better today
than it was immediately after the stroke, however.

My OT had to outspend my PT. She convinced me to
order a device for my hand and wrist that served two purposes. The first thing this device did was keep my fingers
straight, and the second was to get my wrist to bend. This
device was bulky, hard to get on, and a bit painful. It required tightening seven different straps sequentially to get

it on. It seemed like it took fifteen minutes to get in on, and after a half-hour my hand would be numb. I used it a few times but eventually "retired" the use of it.

In addition to these two rather expensive devices, both of the therapists fabricated useful devices for me. These devices were mostly artistic foam covered with black duct tape but were very successful in helping me. Straps were foam and were held in place with the hook part of hook-loop fasteners similar to Velcro.

My OT had made a flat block for retaining my hand with the walker with Velcro straps that I described above. It was not successful with the walker, but by itself was very successful in keeping my fingers flat and extended. I would use this at home for up to an hour at a time, two times a day. I don't use it as often now, but I still use it occasionally.

My PT made a device that functioned exactly like the costly and bulky device that held my fingers flat and my wrist bent backwards. The major difference is that I was able to attach it to my palm first and then bend my wrist afterward. This made it far easier to use and at least as, if not more, effective. I still use this device two or three times a week for an hour or more. My hand, wrist, and fingers always feel much better afterward from being stretched out. I also use my left hand to flex my right fingers throughout the day.

My PT also created a unique device that she figured would help restore movement in my ankle. This device allowed me to flex my ankle and foot from side to side, and, by repositioning it ninety degrees, it allowed me to exercise my ankle forward and backward. Initially, this helped a lot to get this movement back in my ankle and foot. She made this device out of an old Yellow Pages phone book and a piece of one-inch PVC pipe. The phone book was tightly wrapped with duct tape so it was like a block of wood, and the PVC was taped to the bottom lengthwise with duct tape.

Not to be outdone, my OT came up with a device that allowed my arm to gain movement sideways. This device consisted of an adjustable pole to which she attached a flat piece of plastic to one end and a strap around the pole. The object of this device was to put my right hand on the flat piece with the opposite end on the floor and flex my arm outward. The strap was held in my left hand to pull my right back across my body. Of course, I would then move my right arm outward and pull it back again. This device was very simple to make, effective to use, and helped me get lateral or sideways, movement back in my arm.

I mentioned earlier that my PT was a young lady who took every advantage she could of additional training and learning new methods and implementing these methods. I very much appreciated this in her. Because the hospital was only a mile from Tami's house, she came over a half dozen times at no charge to work with me after my insurance benefits expired. There are not that many therapists that will do that, but I had the privilege of having one. Her additional visits helped me to get my arm to swing backward behind my back a bit. That helped me get my belt to go through the loops, at least when I wore dress slacks or jeans.

My insurance benefits eventually lapsed, however, and my outpatient therapy ended along with them. Now it was up to me to continue further improvement on my own. There are a few things I thought up on my own that seemed to be helpful that I will discuss later.

Chapter 6

Home at Tami's, Away from Therapy

M ANY THINGS HAPPENED TO HELP ME IMPROVE MY PHYSICAL ABILITIES AT TAMI'S ONCE I WAS FINISHED WITH MY OUTPATIENT THERAPY. Most of the improvements came naturally, but I really had the desire to do as much as I could to improve. In order for physical improvements to occur naturally, it was necessary to make an honest, disciplined effort. I could not just lie in bed and expect great healing, so I got up and about in the house a lot.

Because it was nearly January when I had checked out of the "five-star" hospital, winter weather kept me indoors at Tami's for the most part . . . at first. When I did get outside, for the first couple of weeks it was to go to therapy. I would also tag along with Tami or Mike for grocery shopping or on occasion to eat out. At first, I felt any other trips would be too hard on Tami, so I avoided going anyplace else other than therapy or shopping with Tami and Mike.

Around the house, though, I was alone during the days that I didn't go to therapy. Therefore, I had to eat and take care of my daily needs. These included things like using the bathroom, brushing my teeth, showering, shaving, getting dressed, and cleaning my room. What I ate during the day was more along the lines of snack-type foods and leftovers from the night before.

Mike normally made a really good meal at night, and there were usually enough leftovers for me to make a lunch out of them the next day. I didn't need much during the day and was used to just the fairly big dinner. Tami used to keep snack items for Emma, and I would get some of them also. These were simple snacks like mini-muffins or Swiss cake rolls, and once in a while we would get some candy orange slices. I would usually try to get a package of Hershey's Dark Miniatures if I would go shopping with them.

Unfortunately, Tami was scared for me to have anything sweet, as she was afraid that it would raise my blood sugar and hurt my diabetes. I had been controlling my sugar levels for years and knew how much sweet food I could consume to keep it high enough to be above minimum blood sugar levels and low enough to be below maximum levels. In addition, I had greatly reduced my A1C levels over the years and was well aware of and religiously practiced eating almost healthy.

There is a general misconception that a diabetic can drink only water and must never eat anything sweet, or it will instantly put you in the hospital. While a diabetic must control intake, he or she can occasionally indulge in sweets. When I first found out that I had type 2 diabetes, I learned that the best way to control it was by counting carbohydrates. At home I could easily control my carbs, generally by watching portion sizes. When traveling, I would eat a very light breakfast and lunch, and for dinner I would eat at restaurants that had a low-carb menu. When traveling, I would take my blood sugar readings every day to make sure I was controlling it. The big trick I found is to just not overdo it in portion size. Tami and I had more than one rather spirited discussion regarding this while I stayed with her.

Food Prep

Preparing food during the day was an interesting experience with one usable hand and essentially one usable leg. While heating leftovers is easy with two hands and full mobility, it takes some effort when you have limited mobility and use of only one hand. In general, Mike would place leftovers on a plate and wrap them with aluminum foil at night after dinner. Thus, all I had to do was stick it in the microwave to heat it up, take it to the table, and eat. Except it was not quite that simple.

The process to reheat things in the microwave involved using my left hand to move the food. I also needed my left hand to move the hemi walker so I could move my body. As a result, I would move the plate as far as I could on the counter, then use the hemi walker to move me, and then move the plate, and do this again and again until I got the food into the microwave. After the food had been warmed, I had to take it out and move it along the countertop to the pass through (opening) above the sink, and on to the dining room table. I would also move whatever I was going to drink at the same time, along with a fork. Using a knife was, and still pretty much is, out of the question. It takes two hands to cut anything with a knife. With one hand it is very difficult even to butter toast. Once I got the food to the pass through, I would walk around to the other side of the pass through and get the food off the counter and put it on the table. After all that, I could sit and eat. With the extra effort, preparing lunch took somewhat longer, but the result was that I could do it and enjoy eating at the table. Of course, when I was done eating, I had to move the dirty dishes back to the kitchen and clean up whatever small mess I had made. Thank goodness for paper plates and a dishwasher.

Opening the wrappers on simple snacks was a problem for me at first. I was used to gripping the wrapper with two hands and tearing the wrapper open. With my right hand not working, this was not possible any longer. Over a few days' time, I learned that a pair of scissors was an easy tool to use to get into a package to get the snacks out. With snacks like Swiss cake rolls or Nutty Bars, I found it best to cut off each end of the package and then make a cut along the length of the package to get to the snack. This would prevent crushing the contents and avoid making a mess. Some candy bars are rigid enough that cutting off the one end and sliding the contents out works well, but for others I still need to cut both ends off and slit the wrappers lengthwise to get the contents out. I have found that it is interesting in so many ways how you can adapt to having the use of one hand.

Scissors are also great for opening a bag of potato chips and similar snack bags. Before my stroke, I could grab the front of the bag in one hand and the back of the bag in the other, and gently pull the bag open. With one usable hand, that is difficult if not impossible, so the scissors work great. Scissors work well for opening envelopes and other types of packaging as well, such as the packaging on microwave popcorn, plastic bags that magazines come in, and such.

Going to the bathroom at home was much easier than in the hospital. I didn't have to wait for the nurse to come and escort me any longer. During the daytime, I would not have any problems at all. At night, while I was sleeping, I often would not wake soon enough and would often wet myself on the way to or in the bathroom. This became less frequent as time went on, and ultimately went away all together when my doctor prescribed medication for me. Pooping was not a problem other than I would go every other day instead of every day before the stroke. The biggest reason for this probably was that I was eating considerably less food after the stroke. I never felt uncomfortable from constipation or diarrhea once I left the hospital. I did feel fortunate for that.

Most of the foods I ate before the stroke tasted just fine afterward. I did get nauseated from spaghetti sauce that was probably too acidic from the tomato content. Because of the nausea, I would limit myself to how much tomato-based food I ate. I did not have the same feelings from eating pizza, though—even homemade pizza with a lot of tomato sauce. At Tami's, Mike would make tacos for Taco Tuesdays nearly every week. Eating tacos with the tomato-based sauce never upset my stomach, either. I now periodically purchase frozen lasagna and the tomato sauce in it never bothers my stomach either, nor does ketchup, but I seldom use much ketchup because of the high sugar content. (You did know that ketchup is relatively high in sugar content, right? Well, it is.)

Chicken on the bone is difficult to eat because it is nearly impossible to get the meat to separate from the bone using just one hand. Chicken wings and legs are OK if not too spicy. I will eat boneless chicken breasts or tenderloins from time to time, and chicken sandwiches at restaurants. BBQ ribs are one of my favorite foods, and I can eat a half a rack from time to time. I have found a place in town that uses a very mild sauce and cooks them to the point that they literally fall off the bone. These are easy to eat with one hand and a fork without making a mess.

I don't eat pork chops on the bone because they are hard to eat with one hand. I buy boneless pork chops and fry them at home. At times I get pork tenderloin sandwiches when I eat out. Beef filets, sirloin steak, rib-eye steaks, or prime rib are, of course, traditional favorites. If I cook these at home, I will use my electric knife to cut them. When I eat them in a restaurant, I will ask the server to have them brought to the table cut from the kitchen. It's worth extra tip money for this service. I like to cook pot roast in my Crock-Pot from time to time. I will slice the roast, of course, with my electric knife. I have also used my Crock-Pot to cook chicken breasts. This will make the chicken very tender and juicy, and I am able to cut it with a fork.

Cutting ham with one hand can be difficult. I have found that my pizza cutter works well to cut ham. I use it for anything from ham steaks to sliced ham to sandwich meat when I cut it for ham and cheese crackers for snacks. I seldom eat fish for personal reasons. I like to bake cakes, brownies, and cookies at times. I use premixed dough for baking cookies and cut it on the score lines with a carving knife instead of trying to break it. Buttering bread and toast is a bit difficult with one hand. I tend to hold the toast in place with my thumb on my right hand, but find it is still difficult at best. As you can see, I have become quite the culinary artist, being on my own since leaving Tami's house long ago.

I should mention that I have successfully mastered the

art of getting peanuts out of the shell with only my left hand. I keep moving the nuts around in my hand to get the shells off them, but do enjoy them very much. Few of my friends with two hands can successfully get peanuts out of the shell with just one hand, so I often "show off" my new "skills" at gatherings.

There are specialized utensils available for the disabled to eat easier. I have not needed to get any of these but have met people who have very successfully used them. I have fortunately been able to use normal utensils to eat with at Tami's house and to cook with when I returned home.

During the past few months, I have heard from several people that I always look nice and dress nice. Little do they know that most of my clothes are five or more years old, and I perform the basic hygiene that everyone should do as part of a daily routine. My basic routine before my stroke included brushing my teeth, shaving, showering, and getting dressed. I discussed my routine in the hospital earlier, so this discussion now is centered on my routine after I left that facility.

Bathroom 301

When I moved into Tami's house, brushing my teeth at first seemed a bit awkward. First of all, I had always brushed my teeth with my right hand (I am right-handed, after all), and that being my affected side, I had to continue to get used to using my left hand. I had enough grip in my right hand to hold the toothpaste tube cap in my right hand and twist the tube with my left hand to take the cap off and put it back on. I kind of had to put the cap end into my right hand, but I made it work. I would put my toothbrush on the counter with the bristles up and squeeze the toothpaste onto it. Before my stroke I would hold the toothbrush in one hand and squeeze the toothpaste onto it with the other. Controlling the toothbrush in my mouth took a little time, but after a few weeks it was second nature.

Shaving with my left hand took more time to get used to, and took much longer to finish. Wetting my beard and lathering it up was different than I was used to with my right hand. My biggest problem was maneuvering my left hand properly to shave my face completely. It did take much longer at first, but eventually it was second nature. I did make a comment to my occupational therapist during one session, and she suggested that I get an electric razor. Tami and I did buy an electric razor and it was much quicker, but not as close of a shave. I used the electric razor mostly for several months until I got used to using my hand razor again.

A very real issue I had to overcome was standing at the sink instead of sitting in front of it in my wheelchair. I wanted to get rid of the wheelchair in the worst way, and the sink in Tami's house was not set up for using it anyway. I could stand at the sink, but found my right leg ever so slowly fatiguing and having to straighten it and resetting my weight on it. I found that I had to remain conscious of this, and after a couple of weeks it became automatic. The only other thing that was readily apparent was that I would fatigue easily; what I could do in a total of twenty minutes pre-stroke now took about forty-five, complete with rest breaks.

While at Tami's house, I would always use the shower seat. As I said earlier, Mike had installed a handheld shower head in the tub to make showering easier for me, and it worked very well for the time I was there. At first, using the shower was as awkward as it had been in the hospital. Complicating the shower chair situation at Tami's was my use of the hemi walker instead of the wheelchair for mobility. We set the shower seat about halfway back in the length of the tub. The seat portion was divided into two sections. The first was approximately the width of the tub, and a shorter wing was hanging outside the tub. This section was used to sit on while I undressed. After undressing, I would slide over to the seat and close the shower curtain. We made two slits in the shower curtain that were spaced out to allow the curtain to fit over the tubing in the seat between the two seat sections. I would push the slits over the tubing and close the curtain. The curtain would be as watertight as a normal curtain is for a person standing in the shower. I'd then take my shower.

After taking a shower, I would open the curtain and slide to the outer section of the seat to dry off. I would usually have a few towels on the floor outside the tub to stand up on while I dried off my buttocks, then use the hemi walker to walk up against the vanity with my buttocks and pull my briefs on. Then I would work my shirt over my head and comb my hair. After my hair was combed, I would move to my bedroom to put on my socks and pants.

Twice while getting out of the shower, I had the unfortunate experiences of losing my footing on the slick floor with my damp feet, and slipping and falling. The first time I had to have help from Tami getting up again. I have to say that having her help me was embarrassing at first. Here I was her sixty-one-year-old father who has always been the one she came to fix things at her house, and now I had to get her help to get off the floor after taking a shower. This experience could have gone one (or both) of two ways. The first would have been to feel sorry for myself and to be scared of ever taking a shower again. Or I could figure out a solution. In as much as I *really* wanted to live a long time and not have to live alone in a cave somewhere, I needed to keep up my appearance and take daily showers. Therefore, I found it necessary to develop an alternate plan so I could keep taking showers. It was simple, really. All I did was lay out a few extra towels on the floor, and keep the hemi walker close by so that I could reach it from the shower seat and have something to support me while standing up, reducing the risk of my again slipping and falling.

By the time I fell while showering a second time, I had built up a fair amount of strength. I was able to get back up using my left arm to pull myself up on the vanity with the help of my legs. No harm was done, not even bruising, so these falls were minor inconveniences. The lesson learned was that I tended to be very careful moving about to avoid stumbling and falling.

There were really two issues that attributed to my being so cautious in my movements. The first was that the two falls could have been very painful. The "could have beens" included everything from sprains to broken bones. Neither of these would have been desirable under any circumstance, much less being so relatively immobile. Second, the falls really hit home with me and showed me just how vulnerable I really was. I had learned this quite well while in the hospital, but these falls had reinforced it. I wasn't advancing as well in my recovery as I had hoped, either. My hopes for recovery were a bit too unrealistic at this point.

The Adventures of Dressing

Getting dressed had become an adventure in the hospital when I had the assistance from the nurses. It became much more of an adventure when I was at Tami's house getting dressed by myself. The best way to describe my getting dressed is that it became, in some ways, more like *getting into* my clothes instead of *putting on* my clothes. This was evident mostly when it came to shirts and socks, and, to some extent, getting my pants on.

I would always start with my briefs. In the "old days," I would hold onto my briefs by bending over with my hands on each side of the waistband, stepping into the leg holes and pulling them up around my waist. After my stroke, I would lean with my buttocks against the vanity and hold my briefs with my left hand in the waistband. I would bend down slightly and hook my right foot into the leg hole and pull my briefs up to about mid-calf on my right leg. I then made sure I was balanced on my right leg with my buttocks against the vanity and put my left leg into the leg hole, put both feet on the floor, and pull them up to my waist, adjusting them around my waist with my left hand. This was (and is) effective, and it only took a little longer to do once I got to the hang of this method.

Putting on a T-shirt was far easier in the "old days." I would put both arms into the arm holes, slide the T-shirt over my head and pull the shirt down with both hands. My new method is to put the shirt over my right hand with my right hand as far into the armhole as I can. Next I put my left arm into the armhole and pull the shirt over my head. Occasionally in the first few months, my right hand would slide out of the armhole and I would have to start over, but that hasn't happened in a long time. After the shirt is over my head, I pull it all the way down with my left hand. It is very common to have the right side of the shirt get bunched up at my shoulder, but it is easy to straighten it out. Before my stroke, I always used a spray antiperspirant, and still do when I wear a T-shirt under a dress shirt. When I wear a golf or polo shirt, I use roll-on antiperspirant. When I would use the spray-on, it would tend to rub off onto the outside of my shirts and leave white marks in front of my stomach. This would obviously require that I change my shirt and start over.

Getting into long-sleeved dress shirts is a different proposition now as well. When I was staying at Tami's house, I would fasten the button on my right sleeve with my left hand like I normally would. My right hand did not have the ability to fasten the button on my left sleeve though. Tami would have to button my left sleeve for me. When I moved back home, I compensated for not being able to button my left sleeve by buttoning it before putting my shirt on and slipping my left hand through the buttoned sleeve. I donated many shirts for which the sleeves were too tight to slide my hand through, but I kept the ones that were workable. On a positive note, I have quite a bit more room in my closet now.

I always put on my socks before my pants poststroke, unless it is warm outside and I wear shorts. To put my feet into my socks, I will hold the sock open with my left hand by placing my thumb into the opening and then hook the opening over my big toe. I will then pull the opening toward the outside of my foot and slide the opening over my toes. Then I will pull the sock onto my foot. It is almost always necessary to twist my sock on my foot and ankle to assure it fits properly on my foot. This method does take a bit longer than holding the sock open with both hands, but it works for me, and as the weeks and months went by, I hardly noticed the extra time at all. My new normal was just becoming normal, period.

Getting into my pants is probably the least-convenient thing for me to do poststroke. It's not the end of the world by any means. I hold my pants with the right side outer seam in my left hand. With my buttocks up against the bed, I will put my right foot into the pant leg. When my foot is all the way through the pant leg, I will stand against the bed in a near vertical position and put my left foot through the pant leg and stand on both legs. Next, I will pull up my pants and tuck my shirt in as much as I can while pulling the pant waist up to my waist. If the pants have an elastic waistband, I will straighten the pants and my shirt and be done.

If my pants have a button and zipper, I will lie on the bed, and pull the waist together with my left hand, then holding the two ends of the waistband together, I will use my left thumb and forefinger to maneuver the button into the button hole. This might take some work (as well as sucking in my belly), but after a few tries it becomes rote. Of course, if the waistband of the pants is too tight, it will be all but impossible, and you may have more room in your closet after donating those pants that are too small. To get the zipper up, I pull up the tab between my thumb and forefinger, while I hold my other fingers against my pants and pull it up. Typically, I will have to make this move three or four times to get the zipper all the way up.

Putting on a belt with one hand can also be done. I can get my belt through the loops to the center of my back; if the next loop is close enough to the center, I can get it, too, with my left hand reaching around behind my back. If it isn't close enough to the center, I will use my left hand from the front by reaching for the belt end and feeding it through the loops with my fingers. I finish up putting on my belt by pulling it through the buckle and buckling it. This takes some practice at first but also becomes second nature in short order.

Shoes are the last thing I put on. In warmer months, when I wear shorts, I almost always wear sandals for the ease of putting them on my feet. If I know I am going to be in a sandy area, I will wear my sneakers. This keeps the sand or small stones from ending up between my feet and the sandals. When I wear sneakers, I tend to tie them loosely. This way I find I can get them off and on again without having to untie and later retie them. As slow as I walk now, this is acceptable as far as I'm concerned. I have another pair of heavy shoes I wear in snowy weather that I tie like this in the winter. Rubber-soled shoes are harder for me to walk in because they tend to grip carpet and concrete surfaces quickly. That is obviously what they are supposed to do when legs work normally.

My right leg doesn't lift properly at times when I walk. After nearly five years, it is getting much better, but it still requires my undivided attention, or I will scuff my foot along. In order to walk easier when I wear jeans or dress pants, I will wear dress shoes with leather soles. My favorite footwear is, believe it or not, cowboy boots. I wear these as much as possible. The leather soles slide a bit on most indoor and outdoor surfaces, and the thicker heels also tend to keep my right foot up and not dragging as much. I always wear my cowboy boots when wearing jeans, and often with dress pants, depending on the occasion. When dress shoes are necessary, I wear leather-soled loafers. Elastic shoe laces are available, but I have not found any locally. Having them does not feel important enough for me to search the Internet for them yet, but I might do that someday.

Something that has always been important to me is having a clean and organized room. Not that I get obsessed with keeping my room at Tami's or the apartment totally spotless, but I have a tendency to keep dirty clothes picked up, my bed made, papers put away, and stuff like that. When I first got to Tami's house after leaving the hospital, I was unable to actually do much. This worked well, as I really couldn't do much to make any kind of mess in the living room or kitchen. We had brought several things from my apartment, including my small, three-drawer dresser, my clothes, and a clothes hamper. Clothing included a couple pairs of jeans, T-shirts, briefs, socks, and pajama pants. Tami had bought me some elastic-waist, warm-up pants while I was in the hospital as well. On another trip, we brought over some file folders and an expandable fabric file holder for these, my label maker for the files, and, most importantly, my letter opener. We brought my desktop computer, my small TV, pillows, nightstand, and a lamp as well.

Over a period of a few weeks, I was able to get my

hanging clothes organized in the closet, with the shirts, pants, and coats hung in separate areas. I got my shoes organized in the closet. With my limited physical abilities, this took some time. I had to lay my clothing on the bed, smooth it out, and get the hangers arranged on them. Then, with one hand, I had to move each piece of clothing around the corner of the bed, and then hang all the clothes in the closet. I really was proud of the work I did once I got the closet organized.

The clothing in my dresser was relatively easy to fold. I would lay the T-shirts on the bed and fold them like I normally would, with my briefs folded into thirds and my socks properly matched. When I did my laundry pre-stroke, hanging up my clothes and folding my underwear and T-shirts would usually take me less than fifteen minutes. Poststroke, preparing and putting away the same amount of clothing took at least an hour and often longer. Needless to say, it was exhausting work and I took a lot of rest breaks. When completed, it was very rewarding to be able to get the work done.

As far as washing my clothes, Tami always did this once a week or so for the first few months. After a couple of months, I developed enough strength to pull the hamper to the laundry and do my own laundry when she and Mike were at work. Dragging the hamper back and forth was not only time-consuming but exhausting as well. I had enough strength in my left arm and hand to pour detergent into the washer, so that was no problem. I also broke my basic rule of sorting my clothes by whites and colors. The detergent Tami used was suitable for mixing clothes, and I never saw the whites come out colored. Another thing I did was get over ironing my clothes. Before I had my stroke, I always ironed my shirts and pants, but with only one usable hand I didn't any more. Ironing really wasn't necessary anyway, thanks to permanent-press fabrics.

I am the kind of person who likes to sleep in my bed with it nicely made on a daily basis. I always liked the bottom sheet stretched tight and my top sheet tucked in tight at the foot of the bed and the blanket or comforter drawn snuggly up to my head. When I made my bed at Tami's house in the morning, I would use my cane to push the covers flat and crawl over the bed to tuck them in as best as I could between the wall and mattress. It wasn't the neatest-appearing job, but it was the best that I could do.

Sleep Positions

Prestroke I would always sleep on my stomach. I would usually fall asleep within a couple of minutes and would seldom move around while sleeping. I know a lot of people can't sleep this way, as they feel too confined with the bed covers tight like this. After I had my stroke, my sleeping habits changed completely. My right arm was no longer flexible enough to bend under my pillow, and it became impossible to sleep on my stomach. I couldn't sleep on my back because my right arm would not be comfortable. I could lie on my left side and let my right arm hang down, but after a few minutes this position would become uncomfortable.

In the end, the position that turned out to be most comfortable for me was to sleep on my right side with my right arm extended outward. This position was just what my therapists did not like; they were afraid that my body weight on my shoulder was not good for recovery. To overcome their fears, I placed a pillow under my side and slept with my head on two pillows. The extra support kept my upper body weight off my shoulder and allowed me to sleep. I seldom was able to sleep for more than a few hours at a time and would read until I got sleepy again. Sleep is one of the most important things that lead to stroke recovery, so I would often nap during the day, and I still do after almost seven years.

Other things relative to my keeping my room organized include my Social Security disability application paperwork and notes, bills for normal living as well as stroke-related bills, and keeping my medications in order and taken. The steps I took to organize these are covered in the chapters related to these important issues.

During one trip we eventually moved my Mustang from my apartment to Tami's house. While it pretty much sat in the driveway, it was an incentive for me to recover enough to drive again. I would go out and periodically start it, and occasionally Mike and I would take it for a ride with him driving it. During my discharge from the hospital, there was nothing said about any driving restrictions. I also read the paperwork from my discharge and my therapists, and there were no comments about not driving. I knew when I first got home that it would be stupid to drive. I did not have the physical strength to drive, and it was not worth the risk. By mid-March, three months after my stroke, I felt strong enough to take the car out of the driveway and ease it around the block. While I could get around the block, it took me a couple of weeks to get comfortable enough to take my left hand off the steering wheel to shift the manual transmission with my left hand. I never really felt totally comfortable doing this, and therefore only drove it on roads with little "crown" in them.

In the next few weeks, my confidence on the upswing, I drove farther on back roads during the daytime. I would drive the few miles to McDonald's for lunch. Eventually, by mid-April, I felt comfortable enough to drive it to our local Friday Cruise-In car show and spent the night back in my apartment again. I swapped it out for my Suburban for the trip back home, but I brought the Mustang back the following week. It felt good driving again. I was very aware both of what I was doing and what the cars around me were doing. I certainly drove only during non-rush hours, when traffic was light, and made sure Tami was well aware of where and when I was driving.

In the middle of May, I was approved for Social Security disability. It was time for me to move back into my apartment full-time. A woman in the same apartment complex was taking care of her brother who had had a stroke, and she offered to help me if I needed her for anything. With Tami's help, I packed everything that was at her place and returned to my apartment. I know she was somehow disappointed, but I knew it was best for all of us.

Chapter 7

Never-Ending Continued Improvement: Home at Last

I SPENT THE SECOND WEEKEND IN MAY AT THE APARTMENT, ARRIVING ON FRIDAY MORNING FOR THE FRIDAY NIGHT CRUISE-IN. I had been coming every Friday night since mid-April. During that time, I would come to the apartment in the late morning on Friday and return to Tami's home on Saturday.

I had thought long and hard about leaving Tami's, and decided that Saturday morning that the time had arrived. I had been approved for Social Security disability. It was enough to live on when combined with a very small pension, but more on financial matters in Chapter 8. I was walking fairly decently, although very slowly. Walking from the car to my apartment didn't wear me out too much. It was time to move back home.

The woman at the apartment building who had offered to help me once I moved in stopped by that Saturday morning. She offered to help me get my things from the Suburban and carry them into my apartment. So I called Tami to make sure she was going to be home to help me move my things from her house to the Suburban. I left for Tami's shortly after noon. Even though Tami's house is only about seven miles away "as the crow flies," it's a forty-five-minute drive because of the local geography, to include placements of bridges over the river that separates us.

When I got to Tami's, she was sitting in the living room reading a book. Mike was at work, and the kids were both gone to their respective other parents (Tami's and Mike's respective exes). We went into "my" room and got everything ready to be placed in the Suburban. Tami is a fairly petite girl, but works out nearly every day and runs a lot. Translated: she is quite strong. She carried my things to the car, and I was ready to leave in about an hour. My decision to return to my apartment was very emotional for both of us. I really don't think Tami thought I was ready to move back, and she was a bit upset that I had decided to go. I hadn't really talked to her about my returning to my apartment, so I'm sure it surprised her. I had started to feel somewhat like a burden to Tami's family, whether or not I actually had been. I also think she was worried about the lady down at the apartment building as well because she did not know this lady.

When I got back home, I retrieved my hand truck from my storage spot and started to move things out of the Suburban. It turned out that the lady wasn't all that much help. She was soon complaining that her back was hurting from all the effort she was making. So, for the rest of the day, I went solo getting things out of my Suburban, on each trip resting before getting another load. That night I watched a movie on DVD and eventually went to bed. By Sunday night I had everything back in its rightful place and, except for not yet having my cable for the computer and TV hooked up, it felt like I was home again.

I had time Sunday night to think long and hard about all the things that had occurred over the previous six months. I was very fortunate to have survived the stroke and to be well on the way to recovery. I had gone from being in a wheelchair to living on my own again. Even with the recovery I had made so far, I realized my abilities were probably never going to come close to what they had been before my stroke. Most importantly, though, I was alive.

Before I go any further in this chapter, I feel that it is important to tell you that I have been on my own now for more than six years. Some of my recovery took place over short time periods, and some has taken a lot longer. Every day, I notice some small ability I now have that I didn't have the week before, although these things are relative. Note, however, that these are small improvements. It's not like I ran ten miles today compared to only nine last week. At my age that will never happen. I am really excited that I am not dragging my right foot anywhere near as much now, for example. Believe it or not, being able to lift my right foot most of the time when I walk took more than four years, but it is still a major improvement, and one that I am very proud of.

I have a place near the door where I keep my cane. I haven't used my cane within the apartment since I returned home six years ago. I am quite proud to be able to say that I have never fallen at my apartment since my stroke. I almost did one time, but caught myself on the back of the couch. When I first started walking again, my pace was very slow; it was nearly impossible to lift my right foot off the ground. For this reason, there are pretty well-defined traffic patterns worn into my carpet. I personally look upon this as a good thing because it is proof that I have been working hard at gaining my mobility. When I vacuum the floors, some of the wear marks go away, but in the high-traffic areas, like in the hallway, they remain as evidence of my continued improvement.

Taking Showers Standing Up

A really big thing for me when I returned to my apartment was being able to take showers standing up again. When I would wash my hair, I had to be careful not to lose my balance if I tipped my head too far back, and turning around when rinsing my hair I had to take it slow. My right leg's strength was slowly coming back, so I learned that if I leaned my shoulder against the shower wall, I felt a lot more stable turning front to rear under the shower. My shower has none of the typical grab bars normally used for handicapped people. The only time I find I need any help is when I get into it. My shower is a fiberglass unit with a good soap tray molded into the shower end that works well to hold onto.

When I get into the shower, I start with my left leg, and don't have any trouble raising it over the side of the tub. Then I raise my right leg over the tub wall. I will get my foot high enough to start over the tub wall, but when I lower my leg into the tub, my foot contacts the inside of the top of the wall. I don't have any problem getting in the shower in this situation, but I have set a goal of getting in without touching the tub wall at all with my right foot. Over the past few months, since setting that goal, I have entered the tub several times without touching the wall. I more often than not still touch the tub wall, but not as much, and the days I don't touch it at all are still exciting. I look at this as another little improvement and victory.

While I don't use my cane at all in my apartment, for three years I would very seldom go outdoors without it. For more than a year I left it in the car when I would go into the nearby convenience store. Ditto for when I visited my daughter, and all day long when I go to my aphasia group. Usually, though, I would still use it in most places. Using the cane generally allows me to move faster. When I walk without my cane, I find that I must be conscious of the movement in my right foot, especially for keeping my balance.

Surfaces

In Chapter 2, I discussed the unevenness of the floor when I first got my wheelchair. Now I find a similar thing in even slightly uneven paved walkways and asphalt parking lots. The walkways in my apartment complex have various textures because of age and even from the differences in how and when they were poured and finished. They range from very smooth to very rough, and from a surface that is flat across the width to a difference of up to an inch side to side.

The garbage dumpster I use is a walk of nearly two hundred feet, and I park my car another seventy-five feet farther away. Just in that distance from the apartment to my car, there are at least eight variations in slope or texture. While these differences were not at all noticeable when I moved here before my stroke, they are now. Most of the differences are now easy to walk on, but I definitely have three areas for which I remain cognizant and careful. The first such area is a rough surface and side slope on a short distance of walkway. When I wear my sandals or sneakers, this surface tends to grab the soles, not allowing my right foot to slide at all. This is not as noticeable with leather soles. The next area of concern is the tapered curb in front of the dumpster. When I have to step up onto this, it is a bit difficult to move my right foot far enough. Interestingly, stair steps don't bother me as much as this curb. The last area in question is the asphalt out to the car. The asphalt slopes down and also from upper right to lower left. Because of this difference in height, the difference in my right foot movement to my left is really noticeable. The neat thing is that although walking to the car is a just a bit difficult, walking from the car to the apartment is much easier in the opposite direction with the slope.

Earlier I mentioned how I used my two-wheeled dolly to move bulky items into the apartment. Seeing as how the dolly made things so much easier when transporting all those items during my move, I also bought a fold-up cart to use in transporting other smaller things such as groceries into and out of the apartment. This not only makes it easier to handle things, but it also reduces the number of trips needed to the car. A really good example is when I go grocery shopping on Wednesdays. On the way out of the apartment, I will load my garbage bag, if I have a full one, as well as milk and soda bottles, into the cart to take them to the dumpster on my way out. When folded, the cart fits nicely into the back of my car. I will place it in there with my four reusable fabric grocery bags on the backseat. Once I get to the store, I carry the bags into the store. When I am done shopping, I put the filled bags on the backseat or floor of the car. When I get home, I load the cart with the heavy bags on the bottom and lighter ones on top. Then I make one trip to the apartment and put my groceries away.

It took me a while to figure it out, but after three years I could carry some items in my left hand and my cane in my right hand. This is great for carry-out food, pizza, and "doggy bags" when I eat out. I will take out my garbage not using my cane if the trash bag gets full on days other than Wednesday. Otherwise, I would generally carry things such as books, my prescriptions, and other miscellaneous purchases in plastic bags in my left hand while using my cane.

I would like to mention a few other things to note about shopping in general. When I go to the grocery store, I am completely comfortable placing my cane in the cart and pushing and steering the cart with my left hand. The cart provides the balance I need to walk through the store. This shopping cart is great to use in other "big box" retailers as well, even if just getting one small item. My little cart I use to bring purchased or other items to or from the car to the apartment is a one-handed cart without need for use of a cane. When I purchase other bulky things, I will get help from store personnel in getting it outside and into the car. The community I live in is absolutely fantastic for providing the assistance. After four years, I figured out which one or two stores don't help me or others out, and I just plain don't shop there any longer. I really don't see how much more such service would cost these stores if they added it. I often see a huge difference in overall product quality, however.

Charting My Groceries

I have made a huge Excel list of the things I buy at the grocery store. I have some 240 items on this list, complete with prices. Each week I decide what I am going to eat for the following week. I then copy and paste the items I am going to buy each week to a second list. Then I print out the short list and base my shopping on that. I try to discipline myself to only get what is on my list, but maybe once a month or so I will get something not on the list. By using the list, I know what I am going to spend each week, and with items that are on sale that particular week, my expenditure is typically quite a bit less than my list indicates. By making my list and buying only what is on the list, I seldom waste food by having it go bad in the refrigerator or pantry. The people at the store I shop at all think my system is great. The lady in my apartment complex I take shopping every week believes it is a waste of time, but I kid her often about having three jars of peanut butter in her pantry any time she looks at it in the store.

In Chapter 6, I discussed doing my laundry at Tami's house and how, for my last few weeks there, I was actually putting my load of clothes into the washer and dryer. I obviously continued to do my laundry at the apartment, but went back to separating the whites and colors. This required that I do more loads, but I could live with it. Along with that, I have my apartment set up with my couch dividing the living room and dining area. This works out for me really well on laundry day because I can put the clothes hamper behind the couch and sort my clothes into whites and colors on the couch.

Be Sure to Make Your Bed

I wash my bed sheets and towels less often than clothes, so one week I do two loads and the next I will do three loads. My washer and dryer are in a small room at the end of my kitchen, so it is a short walk to them from my sorting area on the couch. As most people do, I wash one load, transfer it to the dryer for drying, and then start the washer again with the next load. Once dry, I will sort it when I unload the dryer. I first hang my permanent press shirts, then my golf shirts, then my pants on the couch, and finally my underwear and socks on the table. I place my hanging clothes on the back of my couch to get them on hangers, and then I put the hangers on the edge of my table before I transfer them to the closet. I sit at the table to fold my underwear and T-shirts before putting them away. I pair off my socks on the table and ball them on my lap. This all works well for me and is similar to the method I used before my stroke. The only difference in not being able to use both hands is that it all takes longer.

It takes more time for sure when I strip the bed and wash the sheets. For my first two and a half years after my stroke, I slept on a futon that was mine in the divorce. The futon was several years old but had seldom been slept on. On the plus side, I had paid a fortune for it when I bought it, as it had a very comfortable mattress and strong wood frame. The mattress was quite flexible, so it was easy to bend the mattress and put fitted lower sheets on. On the minus side, it was rather low to the floor. It wasn't a problem for me to get out of but was really low when making it up. Getting the solid-color bottom sheet started the right way is always a gamble to get the sheet side on the correct bed side. This wasn't a problem before my stroke, but it became an annoying diversion after the stroke. I would bend down and start a corner and move to the other end of the bed to hopefully have the correct corner in place. If it was right, all was well; if not, it meant stripping both corners off and starting over. I would have to rest before doing the other side of the bed. After getting the other side of the sheet under the mattress corners, it was time to rest again before folding the top sheet under the foot of the mattress, and then more rest for me before putting on the quilt. I would spend at least ten minutes on each pillow case. Making the bed really took its toll on me, but I was thankful when it was done.

As my abilities started to come back, making the futon became easier, but I still had to rest quite a bit when doing it. In December 2014 I was able to buy a new bed. I bought a queen-sized mattress and box spring. In terms of the "good, better, best" range for rating mattresses, I was not comfortable on either the "good" or "best" models, so I got the "better" version with a ten-year warranty. Before the new bed was delivered, I went to a bedding store and bought a mattress pad, sheets, extra pillow cases, two new down-filled pillows, and a nice-looking comforter. By the time I was done shopping, I had paid almost as much for the bedding as I had for the bed and headboard.

A New Bed

The big day finally came when the new bed was to be delivered. In the morning I managed to get the futon mattress leaned up against a table and disassembled the frame. I carried the two ends, the side slats, and the bagged-up hardware to the Suburban. Once at my apartment, the delivery people carried out the rest of the futon frame and the mattress; then they brought in the new bed and headboard and set it up for me. I made the bed as soon as they left. Things that were different on the new bed were the height of it and the width of the larger mattress. The height of the bed and rigidity of the new mattress made it easier to fit the bottom sheet on. The extra width required that I work the mattress back from the headboard due to the proximity to the nightstands so I would have room to fit the bottom sheet on, and then slide it forward to the headboard.

Moving the mattress back allowed me to stretch the sheet over the corners far easier with one hand. Another advantage with my new sheets was that they were striped, so all I had to do was line up the stripes before tucking in the corners over the mattress. No more having to start over after placing the sheets horizontally when they needed to be placed vertically. Seeing the striped sheets was a real 'duh' moment for me: Why hadn't I thought of this years ago instead of waiting until I was sixty-four, but what the heck. Tucking the top sheet at the end of the bed is still troublesome with one hand, but it's really just a matter of taking more time.

Other than being bulky, the comforter is relatively easy to put on. I know how much should hang over each side of the bed, so I line it up at the headboard and unfold it toward the foot when I change the sheets. The comforter requires a minimum amount of straightening when it's completely put on the bed. Before my stroke, it was easy to make the bed, and it really takes only a few minutes longer now with one hand. The only thing that is still hard is to put the pillowcases on the pillows, but I just take as long is necessary to get this done. At first I was not comfortable getting up on the taller mattress, but that resolved itself in a few days.

In chapter 6, I discussed how hard it was not being able to sleep on my stomach any longer. Eighteen months after my stroke, my right arm would move enough that I could finally maneuver it enough to get it under my pillow and sleep on my stomach again. At first, I would move it upward with my left hand for what seemed like five minutes to get positioned on my stomach, but even then I was not all the way with my chest on the right still not quite flat. Over time, I find I am able to get my chest flat on the bed, and it takes much less effort to get my right arm positioned correctly. At first, I could only sleep a short time this way, but can sleep this way for up to two hours now before it becomes uncomfortable. This sleep position is second nature for me when I nap on the couch for an hour.

Getting Something to Drink

When a person drinks, normally, he or she puts the container to the mouth, takes a mouthful, swallows it, then takes another mouthful and swallows it without taking another breath. Well, the stroke changed my life in that regard—it affected my ability to do this. When I first got home from the hospital, I would always sip whatever I drank. I could sip less than half a mouthful at a time, because that was all I could swallow. Then I would have to bring the container back up to my mouth and repeat the process. This was fairly time consuming, especially if I was thirsty. Finally, one time about twenty-four months after my stroke, I was drinking something when I suddenly realized that I could drink like I had normally been drinking pre-stroke. Drinking properly was not something I had been thinking about or concentrating on in any way, but it just happened. I have been drinking properly ever since. That was just another ah-ha moment like many others.

My right-arm movement, while not great, is much

better in so many ways now. When I first moved back, my elbow was in what seems like a bent position across the front of my stomach. Over time my elbow became more relaxed. While it still is not able to be fully extended at my side when I walk, it is far closer to it than ever. I can get my arm up over my head when I lie on my back on the couch. I can even get it fully extended with my elbow straight for up to twenty-five repetitions. Unfortunately, this motion doesn't transfer to standing and moving my arm. It seems that overcoming gravity while sitting or standing is far harder than I realized.

After close to three years, I finally was able to touch my face with my right arm. It took a lot of concentration and effort, but it was another victory. Two months later, while doing reps of touching my face easily while sitting at my desk, I tried to move my right hand to touch the back of my head. While it took a tremendous effort, I was able to do it. It is now much easier to do. I still find that I have to really concentrate on right-arm positioning. When I think about keeping my right arm straight, it will be straighter. I also find that my right arm is more temperature sensitive when it comes to being straightened. In the winter, I have the heat in my apartment set at seventy-five degrees and my right arm is quite flexible. When I set the heat at seventy, my arm is very uncomfortable and it makes a big difference—my right arm becomes stiffer. In the summer I keep my air conditioning set at seventy-eight degrees. But if I am in an air-conditioned building during the summer with the temperature set at seventy, my arm and shoulder become almost painfully rigid.

In the first four years back in my apartment, I made several additions and upgrades. Many of these upgrades included assembly. When I first returned to the apartment, the lady in my building I have told you about didn't have a vacuum cleaner. Her brother had experienced a stroke and didn't drive; thus she was unable to handle getting to a retailer so she could purchase a vacuum cleaner and have it assembled. So, the three of us went to a "big box" store, where they decided which vacuum they wanted and could afford. We got the vacuum home, and they were puzzled over who was going to assemble it. I told them that I could do it, and I took the time to assemble it for them. When purchasing items like this, it seems that the less expensive it is, the more assembly is required. I spent about an hour and a half assembling the vacuum cleaner for them on the patio of their apartment. The whole time they were in their apartment watching TV and talking. When I was finished, I carried it inside, cleaned up the packaging, and took my tools home.

My Daughter, the Runner

Tami is a runner who has participated in many 5K runs and half-marathons locally and around the Southeast. We once had a 5K run here on Thanksgiving morning for which Tami signed up. I told her and Mike that after the run I would make breakfast for them. I also wanted to hang up some photos that I had retrieved from my storage locker. They agreed to hang them for me before we ate.

On Thanksgiving morning, we got to the 5K starting area in plenty of time before the start of the race. While Tami was getting signed in for the run, Emma, Mike and I started to wander around the starting area and I ran into quite a few people I knew from my membership in the Chamber of Commerce. I introduced Emma and Mike to them. It was cold outside, so we went back to the car to warm up during the race, and by then Emma had met so many people that she asked if "I knew *everyone* who lived in Hendersonville." I told her no, just a few. Later as we were leaving to return home, I ran into some more people I knew, and back at home Emma was just shaking her head.

It only took a few minutes for me to position the pictures and for Mike to drive tacks into the walls. After the dozen pictures were up, I started to make the muffins, bacon, and French toast, while Tami cooked some eggs and helped me a bit. We had a wonderful time, and she helped me in cleaning the kitchen before they left.

Hooking up the cables for computers, speakers, and other peripherals is something I find easy, but quite a bit more time consuming due to my reduced mobility. I did have to replace my wireless printer once. The replacement was to be placed on my credenza, but it was something I could not do alone because of its bulk and my having the use of only one hand. The old printer was smaller, and I got it off, but I needed help getting the new one from the box and positioned.

I called Tami and asked her to come over with a promise that I would buy her lunch. While she was on her way over, I reached under the credenza to unplug the power source. The power source was a transformer that plugged into the wall, combined with a lower-voltage cable that plugged into the transformer and ran into the back of the printer. When I went to unplug the transformer, I found that the cable that connected to the printer had fallen out. I plugged it back in, got on my feet again, and the printer worked just fine. I had talked to the lady across the breezeway and knew that she was having the local Habitat for Humanity people coming later to pick up some items she was donating. The old printer was six years old and the new one was more efficient, so when the people came to pick her items up, I asked if they would be interested in taking the old printer while I explained what had happened. The driver from Habitat positioned the new printer for me and used the new printer box for my donated printer, a few new ink cartridges, and the paperwork that I dug out for him. I reached under the credenza and plugged in the new printer. I finished hooking it up and had just finished programming it when Tami came. I told her what had happened, and she chuckled and we went to lunch.

Getting Some New Stuff

A few months later I had to replace my desktop monitor. When I got the new monitor, I crawled under my table and got it hooked up with no problem, other than the extra time involved. Around this same time I also bought a bookshelf, which now allowed me to get the rest of my reference books out of my storage locker and bring them home for me to use. Like most products similar to this one, the bookshelf had been shipped disassembled in a heavy flat box. The store that I bought it from had shipped it to my apartment, which worked well for me. I unpacked the box on the living room floor, and, after I read the directions, I carried each piece to my bedroom, as I wanted to assemble it into the bookshelf. By the time I had assembled the shelf, I had regained more use of my right arm, although it was still quite limited. It was enough to hold the pieces in place while I assembled the fasteners with my left hand. I got it fully assembled and placed it against the wall. Next, I brought the boxes of books I had gotten from storage into the living room, where I sorted them by subject and filled the shelves.

My desk chair was several years old. The leather was delaminating and the chair was squeaking whenever I would move around in it. It was still functional, so I talked to the apartment maintenance men and asked if they would be interested in having it if I replaced it. It turns out they were in need of another chair as there are three of them and they had only two chairs in their office. I picked out the new chair at the office supply store and had it shipped to the apartment. I wasn't home when the new chair was delivered, but I had made arrangements with the delivery company to leave it under the steps. When I got home, I rolled the box into my apartment. It was heavier than I had expected it to be, but I made it.

After I ate my dinner, I assembled the new chair. Assemblage required that I hold some of the parts in place as best as I could with my right hand while I screwed together the parts with my left hand. It took me about an hour to assemble (longer than normal once again), but it went together well for me. I got all the packaging materials back into the carton and put them in the breezeway. I put the chair at my desk and placed the old one by the doorway for overnight. The next morning, I dragged the carton to the dumpster by the maintenance building and made arrangements for the maintenance guys to pick up the old chair when it quit raining.

As I write this, my most recent purchase that required assembly was to replace my inoperable vacuum. I had purchased my old one as an inexpensive vacuum when I first moved into my apartment after my divorce. It had served me well. Remember how I said that it seemed the lesser the cost of a vacuum cleaner, the more time it took to put together? Well, this time I purchased a very popular model that was on sale. When I got it home, the assembly was very easy, as was the use of the vacuum on my floors.

The new vacuum is much easier to use and does a far better job than the old one. It almost makes me look forward to vacuuming.

My whole purpose of discussing my assembly of the more challenging things that most of us run into is to encourage you to take the time to try assembling things on your own, even if you are not fully able. Assembling furniture, a desktop computer, a printer, or a vacuum can be done with a partially paralyzed hand and a good hand—it is just a bit more difficult than having two good hands. Many things can be assembled when the determination is there. Give it a try.

This summer I want to stain my redwood chairs on the patio. My parents purchased the chairs some fifty years ago, and I know they will last a lot longer. I have also been thinking about replacing my two end tables and the coffee table in my living room with something more stylish and current.

New Wheels

During the winter three years ago, I started investigating what kind of vehicle I would like to buy to replace the Suburban. I had bought the Suburban brand-new in 1994. It was now twenty-one years old with 376,000 miles on it, and it had served me well. It had been very comfortable to drive in, was great for hauling things and towing trailers, and still looked really good. Mechanically, though, it was starting to show its age. The car had a few little things that were in need of repair that were easy to live with, but it had one thing that didn't work that well, and, while I could tolerate this problem, I really would have preferred it to work. As you might have guessed, I'm talking about the air conditioner; it had not worked for two years. Most of my driving was within a few miles from home, so I really could live without it working, but I was feeling stronger and wanted once again to occasionally take my monthly sight-seeing trips. Any repairs to the car would have been more than the car was worth. By late March, I had decided that I really wanted a Ford Edge. In April, I figured out what most used Edges were selling for, the down payment I would need, and how long it would take to save up for it. I even went to the local Ford dealer and looked at a new one. I had projected that I would be able to replace the Suburban late in the fall.

There is a used-car dealer about a half-mile from my apartment that I pass by at least once a day and which sells really good, pretty-high-end used cars. I would glance over at the lot as I drove by to see if they had any Edges on the lot. But as much as they specialized in more-upscale cars and trucks, after about a month they still didn't have what I wanted. Tami and I went out for lunch late on a Saturday afternoon, and on the way past the dealer I saw a silver Edge that had not been there that morning. I told her what I saw and we turned around and went back to look at it. It was a 2010 and really clean, and it had just been put on the lot. Literally, it had every option that could be put on it, like leather seats, automatic climate control, and power everything, including the lift gate. Also, it was equipped with a six-disc CD changer and even two sunroofs. While I was dreaming that it would be nice but far more than I could afford, Tami had been looking at the stickers and said they were only asking $10,800 for it—but it had 158,900 miles on it. The salesman came around for a few minutes and said it had been a local trade for another CUV and the previous owners had picked up their new car Thursday—two days earlier. It had just gotten through their inspections, had the routine maintenance completed, and the emissions inspections done, and it had been washed, cleaned up, and it had been put on the lot an hour earlier. He also said they were about to close for the day.

For the rest of that Saturday, I thought really hard about it and went to look at it again on Sunday when they were closed. I could look in the windows and then I looked really hard for any damage to the body. None was visible from what I could see, except for a few minor scuffs, indicating that it had been traded in just as it was. The dealer had put new high-quality performance tires on it as well. The high mileage didn't bother me, as I only drive about three thousand miles a year anyway.

I decided to go back first thing Monday to see what financing could be arranged. The manager reviewed my situation and said he wanted to check with his lenders to see what they would do for me. I went back home, and in two hours he called and told me he had found a lender. He had also printed out a CARFAX report that showed it was in fact a local owner who had bought it new at the nearby Ford dealer, and that it had never been involved in any accidents. It was one of those vehicle histories that was too good to be true, and if you find one like that you are extremely fortunate.

I went back over to the dealer and the manager had the sales paperwork ready, but we had never discussed down payments or anything earlier so went through the details. He had included a pay-off plan that would cover payments if I lost my income for a short term, but I said if Social Security missed a monthly check we would all be in trouble. He agreed to remove that $600 "insurance" cost. He had written it up as a four-year loan with the only down payment being the small trade value for the Suburban. I asked him to figure it at three years with additional cash down. The payment was reduced further, and I agreed to buy it. I drove the "Silver Bullet" home about an hour later. I thought that I would really miss the Suburban, but was amazed that I didn't.

I take the Edge to the car wash every two weeks at the most. When I get it washed, I always hand dry it, vacuum the interior, and clean it out really well. I have waxed it twice now, and once a month I spray detailer on it and wipe it off to maintain the finish, all while using only my left hand. Getting the new car was almost like making me feel that I had come full circle with my recovery. I was really content to be recovered as much as I was and able to do as much as I could when I would look at what all I'd been through the previous three and a half years.

The day after I got the car, my "shopping partner" called me in the afternoon and asked if I had bought a new car because some silver thing was now occupying the spot where I had parked the Suburban, and she had seen it while walking her dog. I told her what I had done. On Wednesday, she was all excited to ride in it when we went shopping. When we got to the store, she just had to tell everybody what "we" had done, and all about the features and such. As good as I felt about having the car, I never would tell everyone that I had bought it or the details unless asked. But as much as it meant to me, the excitement she showed really made me feel good. The gratification I get out of spending a few hours a week helping someone else is truly amazing. My shopping partner doesn't have a car and is grateful that I take her with me when I go. We have a "standing" time on Wednesday mornings, and both use the senior discount at the store. Our shopping trips are about the only time she gets away from the apartment complex.

I have a standing lunch appointment with a retired friend on Tuesdays. We alternate paying and go to different places most weeks. We also have great conversations as well. About once every two weeks, I will also go and have an early dinner. I will take the book that I am currently reading and enjoy a good meal in a quiet setting. I have other people that I go out to eat with as well. Generally these are people who are former business associates and contacts.

One Friday afternoon I went out to a local, upscale burger place. When I was walking out, there was a gentleman walking in who had similar signs of having had a stroke. I looked at him and said we both looked like we had been going through the same thing. He had paralysis on his right side like I did, but also had aphasia, meaning he had a difficult time expressing his thoughts. We went back inside and had the hostess write each other's contact information out, and we agreed to call each other the next week. He had given me his wife's cell phone number and when she answered it, we had a brief discussion about his stroke. She arranged for us to meet the next Friday at the same place. He brought some information about an aphasia group at a local university and invited me to come with him the next Thursday. I went with him and was welcomed into the group. That was about four years ago, and I am still going.

We have a gentleman in town who has a fantastic classic and muscle car collection in a museum-like setting. He seldom opens it to the public, and very few in town even know about it. One Friday night this past March, he opened it as part of a fundraiser and had hundreds of people attend. While there, I ran across my insurance agent and we walked through it together for almost an hour. She introduced me to quite a few of her fellow Rotary Club members. When we left, she suggested that I join Rotary. I met with her at her office to discuss joining, what the cost would be, and what I could do to participate. After a week or two, I agreed to go with her to a Wednesday breakfast meeting.

That pretty much highlights my then-current social activities after my first three poststroke years, other than with family. I look upon these activities as a very positive part of my recovery and am grateful to be able to participate in them. They give me something positive to look forward to for four or five days a week. I will convey my thoughts on keeping a positive attitude in chapter 11.

Chapter 8

Financial Issues

UNLESS YOU HAVE VERY GOOD HEALTH INSURANCE WITH SHORT- AND LONG-TERM DISABILITY AND VERY GOOD MEDICAL WITH 100 PERCENT COVERAGE AND ZERO CO-PAY AND DEDUCTIBLE, and 100 percent hospitalization, you are not going to escape a stroke without some cost out of your pocket. My total medical bills due to the stroke were in excess of $140,000. I had a decent medical insurance policy with a $5,000 deductible and hospitalization at 80 percent of the remainder after my deductible was paid. I didn't have either short- or long-term disability, or the next level of medical and hospitalization insurance. My employer paid a large part of my insurance, but I still could not afford getting more coverage even with my employer plans. In retrospect, I probably should have scrimped on something else in my monthly budget, but hindsight is always

20/20. By the time all the medical bills were considered, I picked up an additional $32,000 in deductibles in the medical debt just from the stroke.

In many ways, insurance is like gambling. When you sign up for the policy and pay your premiums, you are "betting" that you will one day "win" and the insurance company will "lose" the bet and pay off your expenses, be they medical, auto, life, or home. The insurance company is betting that they won't have to make excessive payments. Insurance companies have people on their staff called actuaries that in some ways are like bookies. The insurance company actuaries determine the "odds" of the coverage you will need, and you are charged accordingly in your monthly premium bills. This is the risk that they accept, and they make sure that the premiums cover the risk and overhead and still allow a profit. Many insurance companies have been around for many years, some for a hundred or more. I "won" some $110,000 from my bet but lost well over $30,000 in additional medical bills, not counting the many additional thousands in lost income. I am, of course, very thankful for what they paid, but in the end would have benefitted more if I had purchased more insurance. I wrote this to give some thoughts on insurance needs.

Because my stroke happened on a Friday, I was only able to collect pay for the previous week that was paid on Friday and for the four days I had worked earlier that week as well. This would be paid the following Friday.

Tami picked up those two checks and deposited them into my checking account. That was my last income I had until June, or almost six months later.

A year before my stroke, I went through a somewhat nasty divorce that had completely drained any accounts I had. I was, literally, living from one lousy paycheck to another. Income from the floor-cleaning business was being spent on equipment leases, supplies, and other overhead items. I had two separate checking accounts: a personal account and a business account. The two lease items for the business were automatic drafts, so all I had to do was make sure I had enough funds available in the business account to cover the monthly drafts. I had already paid my rent for the month before I went to the hospital, but that was all. Normally I was very diligent about my budget and paying bills, but that diligence went out the window when I went into the hospital.

It was obvious while I was in the hospital that I would not be able to return to my apartment for some time, so Tami completed a change of address form to have my mail delivered to her home. She sorted letters and cards from bills and left the bills at home. Cards and letters were nice to have at the hospital. When I was discharged and she went back to work, I went through all of my mail. A lot of the junk mail I could throw right out. I then made three piles. One for bills, one for the company mail, and one that was in reality junk mail that I felt I should open. I read all the junk mail; if no action was necessary,

I tossed it. Next, I sorted the regular bills and medical bills. None of the medical bills showed any insurance payments, so these were put in a separate pile. I was very tired at this point, so I set the whole mail-sorting project aside for that day.

Trimming the Budget 'Fat'

The next day I went through my budget and determined a couple of items that I could eliminate. My ex-wife had agreed to postpone child support payments until I had a source of income again, so it went off the budget. That was nice of her, but she took advantage of my stroke later in other ways. I obviously wasn't driving, so I had no use for gasoline, but I kept my car insurance. I had a budget line for groceries and lunches at work, but seeing as how I wasn't working and was living at Tami's, that line item went away. Finally, I stopped my cable and the telephone landline for the apartment. Believe it or not, canceling the landline phone was the hardest thing for me even though it was the smallest bill. I had had that phone number for more than twenty years, and, in a small way, in losing that number, it hit me that the change I was going through was real. I was able to remove the line items for supplies and overhead from the company accounts as well.

I had a business credit card that I had seldom used that had several thousand dollars of credit available on it. I also had agreed with my bank teller to sign up for a personal credit card; I did this so she could get a bonus. This personal card had an available credit line of eight thousand dollars. I entered both available lines of credit into my budget and extended the new budget out for six months. If I didn't get some income source going by then, I wasn't sure what I would do, but at least I could make things go at least that long. That took a major worry off me.

Tami and I took time to travel to the local Social Security office on the north side of town one day. I had earlier gone online and made an appointment, but the first appointment available was nearly a month away. So, we decided to go without an appointment and take our chances on getting in sometime that day. Once there, we sat in an overly crowded waiting room for nearly an hour, with me in the corner in the wheelchair while Tami found a lone seat in the middle of the room. Because I wanted to talk to a representative about applying for disability, our waiting time was less than it was for others who were there to discuss replacement of cards, missing checks, signing up for retirement benefits, and things like that. Some people told us they had been there for two and a half hours so far. Most of the people who were in the lobby were taken care of at service windows in the lobby. Our number was called within about forty-five minutes, and we were taken to see a representative in the back of the office.

We talked with a nice gentleman, who asked some questions to complete an application form for disability. Obviously, my name, address and Social Security number were needed. He then called up my entire forty-five-year work history on his computer. We briefly discussed what I had done at each job with more emphasis placed on my most recent job. He then did a calculation and gave me an estimate on what my Social Security payments would be if I were approved. He said the process would take five months. Also, I would shortly be assigned a case worker, and the case worker would call in about two weeks to get the next step of my claim started.

He did miss out on two things. The first was the amount that my monthly benefit would be. The amount he came up with turned out to be sixteen dollars more than the actual payment. The second thing he told us was that after the claim was approved, in some cases it would be retroactive to the date of occurrence. After I was approved, I asked my case worker if my first check would be retroactive. She said that all disability claims have a five-month waiting period. The case worker explained that the guy we talked to misspoke regarding retroactive payments. I even checked the Social Security website for disability and verified this. It was possible that the original representative worked in a different specialty area of Social Security that had different rules, as by the time we talked to him, it was lunch time and the office was nearly empty.

Within a week I received a phone call from a pleasant lady from the Chicago office of Social Security. One of my first questions was why, if I lived in Tennessee, I would be working with her and not someone more local to Tennessee. Her response was that the Chicago office would be responsible because it was the office of record from when I originally applied for Social Security when I was ten years old. Over the next three months, she contacted me every week or two seeking information as to how I was progressing and information from my various medical providers. In some situations, she would mail requests and Tami and I would fill out the forms and return them. Other times she needed information that I could provide on the phone. There were also times that I had to take brief notes and I would ask her to hold on while I set the phone down to write my notes. She understood the whole one-hand process very well and would patiently wait for me.

The primary information she needed came from my neurologist, the therapy doctor responsible for my therapy (not the therapists themselves), and my personal physician. She gathered information on my past and most recent job duties, employer, medications, and lab work as well. The process with the Social Security office lasted a bit less than three months. The final step in the process was an appointment with an independent Social Security physician for a separate opinion in April. This appointment lasted all of twenty minutes, during which time the doctor and I discussed my stroke. She also tested my right arm for muscle control and observed me walking. A couple of days later, I received a phone call from my case worker thanking me for going to the appointment and telling me to expect correspondence in the mail. Throughout the whole process, neither my case worker nor anybody else involved in the process ever told me that I would be approved. We just handled the process one step at a time. Eventually when I moved back to my apartment, I purchased a Bluetooth head set to make phone conversations far easier.

Approved

A few days later I received my approval letter in the mail. The letter showed the monthly amount I would receive, and it went on to say when I would start getting paid, and the date and day I could expect my first payment. The letter also summarized the options for payment and instructed me how to inform the Social Security Administration of what method I selected. In subsequent weeks, I received information on when I would be eligible for Medicare and what other pension plans my past employers might have available. I also received a letter that suggested I investigate state programs such as state Medicaid and SNAP (food supplements).

I was eligible to collect Social Security Disability beginning May 1. While I am not going to tell the amount in this or any chapter, I will say it was near the maximum allowed due to my previous work history. I went to my budget file and figured out that if I controlled my finances carefully, I could eventually live on my checks and not be dependent on my credit cards. The biggest drawback is the date I would be paid my first check. Social Security is paid once a month in the month after it is earned. The date is assigned based on your first initial of your last name. For my last name, I get my check direct deposited into my checking account on the third Wednesday of the month. In my case, my deposit for May would come on the third Wednesday of June. The third Wednesday can be a date from the fifteenth of the month to the twenty-first of the month.

During the month of May, I visited the state agencies they had recommended to me to see if I would be eligible for Medicaid or SNAP payments. My SSDI income was too high, and therefore I was not qualified to collect benefits from either program. This meant that I was responsible for paying my own health insurance. At the same time, I contacted the two former employers that Social Security had told me, I might have a pension amount available. I already knew that I had pension benefits available from one of the companies, and I started drawing early on that pension. It's a small amount but everything helps, so I gladly accept it each month. I was quite sure I had nothing available from the second source they had mentioned; in fact, I did not.

About a year after being approved for Social Security, I visited the local office to see what restrictions they placed on supplementing my SSDI income. The representative told me that I could earn up to $9,000 a year. If I earned more than that, I would lose all my SSDI. Not only that, but before I went to work anywhere, even on a limited basis, I would need approval from Social Security. She also told me that when I reached my normal retirement age of sixty-six, any such restrictions would be lifted when I seamlessly was transferred from SSDI to regular Social Security. I sat down at home and thought about what she had told me and decided that I would be much better off not even trying to find a part-time job—not with those restrictions on me. Between the benefits from not only the SSDI income and my pension but also upcoming Medicare benefits, I decided working even part-time was not worth the risk of losing my benefits.

There are basically three programs that pay Social Security benefits. Two of these programs pay benefits from a trust fund that is paid for by our FICA taxes from most of our paychecks. When we work for a company, we pay only half of our FICA tax and our employer pays the other half. If you are self-employed, you are required to pay both halves of FICA taxes. This obviously is an incentive to work for a regular employer. Other employees, such as enlisted military, are covered by the Veterans Administration and are covered by other benefits. Self-employed people include real estate people, sole proprietors, and a multitude of others who get 1099 forms at the end of the year instead of W-2s to show income. Two of the Social Security programs pay benefits from a trust fund created from FICA taxes. The third program pays benefits from funds gathered from general tax revenues.

Supplemental Security Income, or SSI, is designed to help disabled people who have little or no earned-income credit, and it provides cash to meet basic needs for clothing, food, and shelter. This program is funded by general tax revenues. It is used by people who have little work history and few Social Security work credits. This program is used to pay benefits for younger people, spouses who stayed home to care for children or the household, people who worked part time, etc.

The second program is Social Security Disability Insurance, or SSDI. It is paid to those who meet the disability requirements and have the appropriate Social Security work credits and have paid Social Security taxes. The amount paid with SSDI is based on what you would earn at your normal retirement age had you been able to work that long. Generally, after two years, anyone on SSDI will receive health insurance through Medicare. With either SSI or SSDI, the medical requirements for disability payments are the same. Social Security will determine which program you will be eligible for when you apply for disability.

The third program is Social Security Retirement. This is the program everyone who pays into Social Security is eligible for. The reason I mention Social Security Retirement here is that SSDI seamlessly converts to Retirement when you reach the appropriate retirement age. Social Security has many other payment programs available to assist disabled people. These programs include survivor benefits if one spouse dies, spousal benefits for divorced spouses when a marriage lasted over ten years and the spouse never remarried, and benefits for children under eighteen years old. In my case I had adopted my stepson during my third marriage. He was under eighteen when I had my stroke, and even though we were divorced, my ex-wife and stepson collected monthly child-care benefits until he turned eighteen.

There are some short-term disability programs that are specific to certain states. These programs are funded by some states and are independent of any federal government disability programs. Because I lived in Tennessee with no dependents, I was not eligible for any state programs.

Many times a disability claim is denied on the first try. In fact, only about 40 percent of disability claims are approved on the first try. Many of the denied claims are subsequently approved through an appeal process. Claims are denied for many reasons, but denial for true-disability claims is normally due to insufficient or inaccurate information being provided to Social Security. Quite often people use a lawyer to assist them in filing claims or appeals.

In my situation I developed a great relationship with my case worker. I explained to her the physical problems I had walking, the limited physical use of my right hand and arm, and how much my speech had been affected. I was very careful not to either exaggerate or downplay my disabilities. She obviously could hear my speech difficulties over the phone, and the fact that I had to set the phone down to take notes indicated to some extent the problems with my right arm and hand. I was always cordial and honest with her. I very much avoided giving her any indication that I saw ours as an antagonistic relationship. I am convinced that this made her easier to work with and more willing to help.

I also placed a great deal of trust in all of my doctors, therapists, and nurses in the hospital. If any of them told me something I did not understand, I would get clarification right away; I didn't worry that asking a particular question might make me look like a dummy. A doctor studies for years to practice his trade, as do most of us. The same doctor that fully understands the care he practices could probably never understand engineering terms or stresses on a piece of steel as well as I do, or have the same abilities I developed in my second career in sales.

A good example might be something that I experienced when I was younger. When I built my second house, one of the best doctors in his specialty in town had a house built in the same subdivision. One day I drove past his house, and he was standing out in front trying to put up a mailbox and was totally perplexed. I stopped and asked if I could help. He followed my instructions in assembling the box to the post, digging the hole, and filling it back in around the mailbox. He had a lot of questions about putting in the mailbox because it was something he didn't know. Similarly, I asked my doctors questions about my stroke because it was something new to me, and I did-n't know anything about it.

My medical records indicated in great detail what de-ficiencies I had as a result of my stroke. My doctors prop-erly documented everything. Not only that, they all handled requests for information from Social Security in a timely manner, and that information was easily under-stood as well. Throughout the process of my initial recov-ery, I had many follow-up appointments with my doctors before my initial claim was approved. I asked a lot of ques-tions during that time, and am sure that my doctors noted my questions. This had to help when they submitted my medical records to Social Security.

I looked at receiving Social Security Disability and my small pension as another positive step in my recovery. It was just in time to allow me to pay rent on my apartment again, pay my utility bills and insurance, and buy gro-ceries and gas. It also allowed me to start my child support and leases for my business again. I have to say that it was a bare-bones budget with just a few dollars for groceries every month. There were no funds available for medical bills from the stroke or for paying off the credit cards that I used to live off for the past six months.

Bankruptcy

The biggest asset I had was my beloved Mustang. The Sub-urban was worth a thousand dollars, and my tools were worth maybe a thousand dollars. Household assets were worth another thousand dollars. My debts were someplace near six times my assets. The only way out was to file bankruptcy. After meeting with a bankruptcy attorney, I learned what I could keep and what I would have to sell off. I ended up selling my Mustang and paying off my local doctors and some other debt. The rest of the medical, personal, and business debt went into the bankruptcy.

The bankruptcy cost $1,400, and it was paid in five payments. The lawyer needed $300 to start the process and then four monthly payments of $275. It took me nearly two months to come up with $300 to get the bankruptcy started. I had made a spreadsheet of all the individual creditors, account numbers, and amounts I owed, so the interaction with the attorney in filing was quite brief. The actual court appearance with the judge lasted about ten minutes and was handled by an associate of my lawyer. The judge wanted to know about my assets, in particular what had happened to the Mustang. I told him that I sold it and paid off several bills, and he wanted to check into it himself, so the bankruptcy was not granted in my first appearance.

The day in court was not what I needed. Here I was with the highest unsecured debt in my life other than past home mortgages, which were really secured debts. I did not have any gainful employment to provide income, and I did not have the physical ability to seek a job. Add to that my meeting with Social Security, when I found out about the restrictions they imposed. Finally, I had heard of other cases that day in which other people there were seeking second and third bankruptcies in two years, had far more assets and had gainful employment and were granted a second bankruptcy. This day was absolutely the worst day I had ever experienced in my life.

About a month later, I received a letter from my attorney that the bankruptcy had been granted. This letter was just in time to pay my first payment to my attorney. I went to see my attorney to see what I had to do next, and she told me that each creditor had been sent a letter and that if I was contacted by any of them, I should have them contact her. I wanted to know about the leased equipment for the business and she really didn't have an answer. I waited a week or so and called each of the lease holders.

Two of the lease agreements were for small pieces of equipment, and those lease holders sent me boxes and packaging to ship the equipment back to them. The third lease holder was for the bulk of my equipment and would require crating and truck shipping. The lady I talked to at the leasing company told me that she would have to get back to me as far as a disposition. Two weeks later, I contacted her and she told me that they did not need anything back and I could do anything with the equipment that I felt appropriate. I had kept in touch with a couple who had gone through the equipment training with me and were thinking about expanding their business to see if they would be interested in it and they were. They offered me a thousand dollars for the equipment along with my small inventory of supplies, so I took them up on it. Two weeks later, they picked it up. All I had left of the business now was the trailer I had used to transport my equipment to jobsites. I owned the trailer outright. Two weeks later, a friend offered to buy it from me. The final chapter in my business had come to an end, and the happy dreams about it that I had were no more.

Unexpected Payout

Throughout this process of the bankruptcy and closing the business, I did have some good fortune. First of all, my former employer kept my health insurance coverage going for me for nearly a year. I went and paid the employee amount every month, and they paid the rest. This was really great for me and saved me a ton of money when I really needed it. The second was a few hundred dollars that I never expected. My grandfather had bought the mineral rights to some land in Canada as well as some in North Dakota in the 1950s. These rights had been passed down to my mother and two of her sisters. When they died, the rights went further down to my brother and sister and me, and three cousins. The company that owned a lease on the Canadian mineral rights sold the lease to another company. The new company paid each of us a fee to update the lease on our mineral rights. It was the first time that I can remember anyone in the family earning anything from this in almost seventy years, and the money came to me when I could really use it.

Health Insurance

Health insurance was definitely a major need after I had my stroke. I was concerned that without getting the physical exercise I had been getting, and with my age, that these were going to be problems factoring into my health going forward. As I said earlier, my former employer carried my insurance for the first year and the coverage was greatly appreciated. It freed up enough money for me to pay off my child-support obligation and maintain myself as well. However, like all good things, my employer-based insurance would not last forever, and I was put onto a COBRA plan one year later.

The COBRA plan raised my monthly health insurance cost from $86 to $416. COBRA essentially is a plan that an employer must provide to any former employee to allow that employee to retain group health insurance coverage. The full cost of this insurance is the responsibility of the former employee. As such, I paid the premiums to the company's insurance agent rather to my former employer. The biggest advantage of COBRA is that my insurance was provided as part of my former employer's group rate rather than a policy written for an individual. Group rates are typically considerably lower than individual rates because the insurance company spreads their risk over more people in the group, hence the group members save money on the policy. COBRA coverage must be offered for eighteen months from the day employment is terminated.

Normally, by keeping my insurance coverage active for a year after my stroke before changing it to COBRA coverage for the next eighteen months, I should have been covered up to the time my Medicare coverage became effective. In January 2014 the insurance provisions of the Affordable Care Act (Obamacare) became effective. This change caused insurers to reset their rates for all coverage due to the higher risks they determined would come with the new program. The company negotiated a new rate with their insurance carrier for their annual health policy. My COBRA coverage was going to be increased from $416 a month to $539.

I received a letter in December of 2013 from the insurance agent that announced this increase. The letter also said to call them and see what other alternative coverage was available. I called and set an appointment to see a noncommercial agent at the agency the Friday before Christmas. He had been told what my needs were before I arrived, and we immediately went to the ACA sheets. The sheets we used showed several plans available from two different carriers, and we selected the plan that afforded me similar coverage to what I had through the group. With the plan, I could keep my doctor and the hospitals that I had been going to. The plan would have cost me just under $300 a month after the credits from the government were applied to it.

We logged onto the ACA website and started to input my information. After some time, we were kicked off the website and could not get logged back on to it. After several attempts, we decided to contact a navigator by phone. When we got a navigator on the line, we explained how we had started our application and been booted off by the system. She checked the ACA website for our application and was booted off as well. By this time it was closing time for the agency, so we set an appointment for after the holidays, January 2, 2014, when we could resume my application. After three and a half hours, we were basically no further along with my application than when we started.

The next time we met, we were able to log onto the ACA website and retrieve my application as far as we had gotten. We had gotten to the point of putting the information describing the plan we had selected, and the website said it was not available and to select another plan option. The options that were now available were either way more expensive or offered reduced coverage. My primary physician was on the approved list for the lower-level plan, but none of the hospitals I had used in the recent past were included. The next higher plan was far more expensive, and the deductibles were higher than I had previously, but at least I could get care at my recent hospitals. I reluctantly selected the least-expensive plan, hoping that I would be healthy for the next five months until my Medicare coverage started. In essence, the plan we selected had cost the same as my former COBRA coverage before the government credits were taken into consideration, but it had a higher co-pay for doctors' appointments, had deductibles that were $10,000 a year, and the nearest hospital I could use was in the next city and was some twelve miles away. Fortunately, I never had to use the ACA insurance before my Medicare coverage kicked in.

Medicare

When my Medicare coverage was about to start, I researched the supplemental-coverage options. There were four companies that offered coverage in my area. One of the companies I ruled out immediately because I knew a person who had it. The coverage she had was not as good as others, and I knew my doctor would not take it. The second company I looked at was a smaller company and had limited providers that did not include my doctor either. That left two that, on the surface, looked comparable. I had a very close friendship with my hospital's accounting person, so I asked her which insurance she preferred. I also stopped by my doctor and asked which they preferred. Both my friend and the doctor recommended the same insurance, so my decision was made. In different areas and situations, another company might be a better selection. It is important to talk to all of your medical care providers when you make a decision as to which supplemental coverage to use.

Medicare is really great health insurance for me. My Medicare premium is deducted from my Social Security check and the Social Security Administration forwards this money to my insurance company, making it seamless to me. In addition, my coverage includes a visit to my doctor every three months as part of my wellness plan. My insurance company's wellness plan includes semiannual home visits by insurance company doctors to review my wellness activities, and periodic additional visits such as eye retina tests. A nice incentive that I get with the wellness plan are the gift cards I can get from them. My Medicare plan also has a great co-pay benefit for office visits, and it has a good co-pay for prescriptions as well. Since the insurance supplement is tied to prevention, it also has an annual membership in a fitness facility.

I had a medical need while I was covered under the COBRA policy. On a regularly scheduled visit to my doctor, I told her that I had been low on energy and had been sleeping what I considered to be too much. She drew a blood sample, and she called me the next day to tell me my red blood cell count was at 5.0 when it should be a minimum of 12.5. She wanted to do a stool sample to see if there was any internal bleeding. When my stool sample showed slight internal bleeding, she sent me to a specialist. He scheduled a colonoscopy to see if the blood loss could be explained. Prior to the colonoscopy, though, he scheduled a blood transfusion with three units of blood. He wanted my blood count to be at least close to normal before the colonoscopy. Three units is a lot of blood to be transfused. In fact, the blood transfusion was started at about 10 A.M. and I was in the hospital until 6 P.M. when the last bag was completed. The nurse than checked my blood pressure and heart rate and found it to be acceptable, so I was released to go home. The drive home was uneventful; however, I did feel that I was somewhat in a bit of a fog. After a few days I really felt a lot more energetic and almost normal again. It was weird how my blood count had dropped over a period of time, and I didn't really notice a drastic change in my energy levels that the low red-cell count indicated I should have felt.

Colonoscopy

A few weeks later, I arrived at the hospital for the colonoscopy. This time I had Tami bring me there and home. Afterward, my doctor told me that the colonoscopy indicated no problems, and he put me on an over-the-counter, 350-milligram daily iron regimen. My doctor and I discussed my physical activity (which obviously was not much), my sleep patterns, and my diet. When I told him that I had for all intents and purposes cut red meat from my diet for the past few months in favor of chicken, turkey, ham, and occasional pork, he told me that red meat at least twice a week was necessary as well as more salad. By changing my diet as we discussed and taking the iron pills along with the blood transfusion, my next blood workup showed my red cell count had gone up to an acceptable number, and that I should keep up with the changes.

When Tami and I had arrived at the hospital for my colonoscopy, they had checked my insurance and suggested that we pay upfront for the procedure. The cost if we paid upfront would be about $1,800. I surely didn't have $1,800 lying around, so I declined. When I got the bills from the hospital, the bill for their portion was for $2,400.

The doctor bills were much less, so I was not worried about paying them at all. The lab bills were less than a hundred dollars and the anesthesiologist was about the same. I paid the lab and anesthesiologist in full. I worked out a plan with the doctor to pay off that bill in three payments. That left the hospital. I met with the receivables person there and we worked out a plan that I agreed to $100 a month; if I could pay it off early, she might be able to reduce the overall amount. I made monthly payments simultaneously with the doctors, and when they were finally paid, I saved the money each month. After I had paid what I hoped would be the total, the receivables person and I sat down again and she recalculated the bill. In the end, I paid just a bit less than the original $1,800. I really wanted to take her out to dinner for working the entire thing out, but never did offer to do that. Her husband probably would not have appreciated that anyway.

It is amazing to me what a person can do to save money when there isa true need. I spent a relatively little time to make the financial decisions I made with the hospital for this visit and the care they provided. In the end, I had to make sacrifices, but I went to bed each night without having to worry about how I was going to pay the bills. I said that I had to make sacrifices to pay these bills, and I made several. Things I sacrificed on were items like buying generics when possible at the grocery store, staying home more and saving gas, and not going out to eat at all and things like that. During the time I was paying these bills, my calculations showed that I was paying nearly 40 percent of my monthly income for health care when I included insurance, prescriptions, doctor bills, and hospital bills.

As I said earlier, my Social Security and my small pension provide a comfortable income for me. It's now been six years since my stroke and I have a decent lifestyle that allows me to have a good vehicle to drive what little I do, provides me decent entertainment, and allows me to go out to eat a couple of times a week. I have my weekly service club meetings and activities, and spend time many months a year helping people who are also stroke survivors. Each month I am even saving a little bit. I really am comfortable with my life now. I really deep down would like more, but if it doesn't come, I could live like I do for the rest of my life and be comfortable.

Chapter 9

The Brain and Stroke

I WOKE UP ONE MORNING ALL EXCITED TO START THIS CHAP-TER. Then I got wrapped up in a couple of articles about the brain, how it works, rewiring it through neuro-plasticity, and topics like that. I decided to save those articles and study them later. They might very well become the subject for another book someday. I intended for this book to be read and understood by real people who didn't have a doctorate in neurology, or an M.B.A, or, for that matter, even a bachelor's degree. This book is intended for people who have had a stroke (or for their caregivers) and to be a quick and easy read. I also intended this book to provide inspiration and to show that just because you had a stroke, it doesn't mean that you have arrived at the end of the world. There is life after a stroke, and it can be lived and enjoyed as much as, if not more than, before you had your stroke.

Just like we have different faces, heights, weights, fingerprints, teeth, or any other source of comparison, we all have different brains. Just as we all have different shapes to our faces and heads, our brains have different shapes. This doesn't necessarily mean that these differences have any kind of impact on how smart or dumb you are. These differences give us each a sense of individualism. When you see textbook pictures that show a brain, the photo generally represents what your brain looks like. An MRI scan of your individual brain is unique to you. It is yours and yours alone.

When I was a kid, which almost qualifies as ancient history, we knew far less than we do now about the brain and how it does what it does to make us living, breathing, walking, and thinking individuals. In the fifty-some years since I was a kid, the world has learned a whole lot about the brain. And just as we know more about the brain, we also know a lot more about strokes. We have really good ideas of what causes them and what to do to prevent them. Yet, as we know more about strokes today, there is an awful lot more to learn.

Strokes

A stroke is also called a "brain attack" or a "cerebrovascular accident" or CVA. Stroke is the third-most-prevalent cause of disability in the United States. In the US there are approximately 795,000 strokes annually. Of these, about 16 percent are fatal. Most strokes are first-time strokes for those individuals, but about 25 percent are in people who have previously had a stroke. Thirty-four percent, or a third, of strokes occur in people under the age of sixty-five. Unlike heart attacks, which fall into one of a dozen or fewer types, each of those 795,000 strokes is, literally, different from all the rest. Surgery is not possible for many if not most strokes, and many strokes lead to long-term disability. Disability can last a few months through many years, and might even be a permanent situation.

A stroke is caused when part of the brain in a specific area is deprived of blood flow. When the blood flow is blocked, the brain cells in that area are deprived of oxygen and subsequently die. The severity of a stroke depends on how many cells were deprived of blood flow and where in the brain the blood flow stoppage occurred.

Typically, all strokes can be classified into two groups—hemorrhagic and ischemic. Another type of stroke called transient ischemic attacks (TIA) is actually a subgroup of ischemic strokes.

Hemorrhagic strokes are caused when a blood vessel in the brain bursts. Blood subsequently flows out of the vessel, starving that area of the brain "downstream" of the burst area of oxygen and nutrients needed for the brain to function. Hemorrhagic strokes account for approximately 13 percent of all strokes, and are fatal in about 80 percent of the people who have them. Depending on the

affected area in the brain, part of the skull might be removed during surgery to repair the bleeding blood vessel.
The section of skull is stored in another part of the body,
such as the abdomen, to keep it alive over the period of
time the vessel healing process is taking place. Most often,
that segment of skull is ultimately reinserted in the head,
when appropriate.

The other 87 percent of strokes are ischemic. Only
about 20 percent of ischemic strokes are fatal, meaning the
chances of surviving an ischemic stroke are much better
than a surviving a hemorrhagic stroke. An ischemic stroke
is caused when a blood clot forms in a blood vessel in the
brain and the clot stops blood from flowing. The area of the
brain downstream of the clot doesn't get the oxygen and
nutrients needed to sustain life in the affected area, and that
area of the brain essentially dies. Many ischemic strokes are
considered massive strokes and result in some form of disability up to and including permanent disability.

Then there's "transient ischemic attacks" or TIAs, a subgroup of ischemic strokes and a type of stroke that has far-
lesser effects than an actual ischemic stroke. This is like a
temporary stroke. A TIA might last from a half-hour up to
about twenty-four hours, and most of the time has no long-
lasting effects on any of the brain's or body's functions. TIAs
are often called ministrokes. Approximately half of all TIAs
leave little to no evidence visible on CT scans or MRIs even.
The other half leave small indications on CT scans or MRIs,
showing that such an event has occurred. Most people who

have experienced TIAs never seek treatment for them due to the lack of long-term effects.

Immediate Treatment for Strokes

Currently, there is no emergency room treatment available to counteract hemorrhagic strokes. The primary treatment for this type of stroke is to control the internal bleeding and then, ultimately, perform surgery to repair the affected blood vessels.

There is a drug that can be administered to victims of an ischemic stroke. This drug is tissue plasminogen activator, or tPA, which is administered intravenously (via an IV). The drug dissolves the clot (a process known as clot busting) and restores blood flow to the affected area. It can do this and leave relatively little or no long-lasting effects. The downside is that tPA must be administered within three hours of the onset of as stroke, although it has been successfully used in some patients up to four and a half hours later. Even if tPA is administered within the three-hour window, it is only effective in approximately 40 percent of the cases. Unfortunately, most stroke victims don't realize what is happening to them, so they don't get to the hospital in time for it to be administered.

The Brain

Your brain, basically, is comprised of two sides inside your skull. We know that thought processes are different between the two halves of the brain in areas such as emotions, logical thought, math abilities, artistic abilities, creativity, and many other things. As far as muscle and movement control are concerned, the right side of the brain controls the left side of the body and the left side controls the right side of the body.

The three most common symptoms of a stroke can be put into a chart with a fourth letter added to spell out the word "FAST," which relates to how quickly you or a loved one should respond to an apparent stroke episode as depicted in the first three letters:

F: Facial droop on one side of the face
A: Arm weakness or numbness on one side
S: Speech difficulty, such as slurred or weak speaking
T: Time to call 911 or get to an emergency room

Facial droop can be seen as an obvious difference in the appearance between the eyes or unevenness in the mouth. An example of drooping in the mouth is when one side can be made to rise as in a smile but the other side won't rise or is actually curling downward. One eye might open fully and the other might not. Differences might also be seen in the forehead and cheeks as a difference in symmetry from one side to the other.

Arm weakness or numbness is another sign of a stroke. This can extend to the hand or fingers. The arm might not be able to bend as much as the unaffected arm. One arm might not have the same range of motion as the other—it may not be able to reach as high, for example.

Numbness might feel as though the arm has fallen asleep, such as when the dentist "numbs" your teeth to work on them. Weakness might also show up in a leg before it shows up in the arm.

Speech becomes difficult for a person going through a stroke. Speech typically becomes slurred, almost as though the person is intoxicated. In addition, the voice can weaken in various degrees. At the worst, the person might not be able to speak at all.

If any of these symptoms occur, it is time to get to an emergency room as quickly as possible. In some cases, as I discussed earlier, the drug tPA can be administered to dissolve the clot and minimize the long-term effects of a stroke.

Additional symptoms to be very worried about are sudden lethargy or fatigue. Either of these can indicate that you are experiencing a stroke. This fatigue is especially important to be aware of when it comes during a period when you normally wouldn't expect it.

A stroke can have an effect on your vision when it first comes on. In a normal situation, both eyes work together to focus and provide vision. When a stroke strikes one side of the brain, the eyes might not work together any longer, and the result is double vision. Another vision-related symptom is the loss of part of your vision in one or both eyes. This would show up as a blank spot or area.

Depending on where a stroke is located in your brain, you might lose some or all cognitive function. Often the loss of cognitive function will be similar to light-headed-ness and will come on very suddenly. It may seem as though you aren't able to comprehend what is taking place around you or that you can't put your thoughts together.

A sudden headache also might be a sign of a stroke. Such a headache will most likely feel as though it is only on one side of your head. If you experience any of these events that seem to be very unusual, it might indicate a stroke, and a doctor should diagnose the cause as soon as possible.

My stroke was what my neurologist called an evolving stroke. Even though I went to the emergency room that Friday morning, I know in retrospect it started the day before, that Thursday. On Thursday morning I went to work and started off the day with our eight o'clock morn-ing sales meeting. When I left the meeting and walked back to my office, everything seemed normal. I read my email, made my follow-up phone calls, and made sure my paperwork from the previous days was complete by nine or so. The weather was lousy, so there were no customers coming in. I sat at my desk with one eye on the Internet and one on the lot, as did the other twelve new car sales-people.

A car salesman has a tough job. At a big dealership like the one at which I was working, the number of sales-people is the number needed to handle every potential customer that might come in on the one or two busiest days of the year. You have to be ready, and staffing has to be in place. That means an individual salesperson has a lot of nonproductive time. Sure, there is a lot of training time that the manufacturer requires, but that amounts to no more than two or three hours a week, if done efficiently. The dealership required other training programs, but they involved minimal time as well. I would usually have this all done very early in the week. It takes two to three hours to sell a car. Very few people sell one car a day. In fact, our "top producers" seldom sold more than fifteen in a month. Fifteen cars a month means forty-five hours of "productive" work a month, out of the two hundred or more hours a month you are required to work at most dealerships. This all means that a car salesperson has well over a hundred hours a month with literally nothing to do. It is a boring, sedentary job, which leads to a high degree of turnover.

Although I went through all this early in this book, I'm going to go back through in detailing the onset of my stroke, now that I've just gotten done explaining the basic science of the brain and how strokes work. Hopefully, this review will now have more meaning to you. That Thursday morning was probably the slowest day I had had in six months. I was so bored that I first noticed something might be physically wrong with me when I experienced some foot dragging while walking to my car at lunch time. That evening I was going to meet several family members for my granddaughter's birthday party, so the anticipation of that made the afternoon go by a little quicker. At about four o'clock, I actually saw a potential customer on the lot, and no one else saw him so I went out to greet him. The potential customer turned out to be one that was only dreaming and, while I did get his name, he wouldn't give me his phone number so I could later call him to follow-up on his visit. At this time, I noticed my right foot was giving me more trouble, so I was really glad to sit down when I got back inside.

A short time later, I left work, stopped to get a birthday card, and went to meet the family at the party venue. I found walking through the store and getting the card hard to do, but just figured I was tired. After dinner at the restaurant, I found myself stumbling. Someone at the party asked me if I was all right. I just said I was tired and that my foot had just snagged on the carpet. I made it out to the car afterward but was having a really hard time walking. I made the twenty-minute drive home and made it into the apartment. Then I got ready for bed and watched the ten o'clock news, and fell right to sleep. I also remember that I had felt a little "buzzed" at the card shop and again at the restaurant, although I had only Coke to drink. I had not consumed any alcohol in at least a year.

I woke up at about seven on Friday morning, which to me was like sleeping in. I was off work that day and had nothing planned for the day in terms of going out, which in itself was very unusual. When I got out of bed, I had a little trouble with my balance, but it was nothing that bothered me. I watched the news for a few minutes and then I was going to work on my resumé that morning, mostly updating it. Before I did that, though, I thought I would take a shower and that it would make me feel better. So I brushed my teeth, shaved, and stepped into the shower. It was while I was in the shower that it really hit me that something major was wrong. I went to wash my hair and couldn't lift up my right arm to wash it. I washed it with my left hand only, and finished my shower. I got dried off and called Tami and asked her to come and get me. While I was waiting for her, I got dressed with little difficulty and even took the garbage out. When we got to the hospital an hour later, the receptionist recognized the symptoms she saw in me as a stroke, and she had me in a room in the ER within about five minutes.

Again, the reason I again wrote all of that was to go back over what signs I had that indicating I was having a stroke. One of the key signs of a stroke is sudden lethargy, or fatigue. Throughout the day Thursday, I had felt somewhat fatigued, but it was not something really sudden or unexplained—I had a very boring, sedentary day. I never lost any real cognitive functions during the day Thursday, until the time I was in the card shop, but by the time of the party a bit later, I felt good again. I was able to keep up with the conversation as I normally would. I felt good driving home but, like I said, I felt a little "buzz" in my mind—similar to the kind of buzz when you've had a little alcohol, maybe a couple beers. I had no vision problems and no headache. I also did not feel any aches or pains anywhere in my body. I was able to eat a steak dinner at the birthday party normally with my right, or dominant, hand as though nothing was wrong. The main symptom I experienced was the very slow onset of the loss of movement in my right leg. It took me nearly twenty-four hours to notice any effects in my arm, and that was only when fully extended upward.

In retrospect I should have paid attention more than I did, especially late Thursday afternoon and that evening. I had really wanted to go to Emma's birthday party in the worst way. On the other hand, I knew little about the signs of a stroke. Even had I known all this information about strokes, I might still have no done anything until Friday morning, as if being in denial or rationalizing that I was OK. Either way, what happened then cannot be undone. I discussed this with the ER doctor and with my neurologist, and they both said my stroke came on so gradually that I did what they both would have expected, and I felt somewhat better hearing that. I just hope that someone reading this can learn from my errors or at least pass this information along to someone that not all strokes have the same catastrophic symptoms.

Chapter 10

Causes, Medications, and Preventing Another Stroke

S TROKES ARE USUALLY ATTRIBUTED TO COMMON CAUSES RELATIVE TO POTENTIAL CIRCULATORY PROBLEMS. These can cause weakening in the artery or blood vessel walls in the brain and lead to blood clots blocking the arteries and blood vessels in the brain. Of course, there is also blood vessel wall weakness which can cause the vessel to burst. I have listed common causes of problems in the circulatory system in this chapter.

Diabetes can be a major cause of stroke. Our bodies use blood sugar, also called glucose, to provide the energy that allows us to function. Glucose is distributed to the cells throughout our body via the bloodstream, and it enters our cells with a hormone called insulin, which is produced by our pancreas. If you have type 1 diabetes, your pancreas does not produce insulin to allow glucose to enter your cells in the form of energy. If you have type 2 diabetes, your pancreas produces too little insulin for the cells in the muscles, liver, and fat to use insulin properly. Your pancreas tries to create more insulin, but over time it can't make enough insulin to keep glucose levels normal. Type 2 diabetes can be controlled with lifestyle changes such as exercise or diet, medications or by taking insulin. Type 1 diabetes requires that you take insulin.

When insulin levels aren't correct, you can end up with too much glucose in your blood and your cells won't receive enough energy. Eventually, high glucose can lead to increased fatty deposits or clots on the inside of your blood vessel walls. The clots can narrow or block the blood vessels in your brain or neck. If the blood clots end up cutting off the blood supply, they will stop oxygen from getting to the brain, causing a stroke.

In 2006, my employer requested that I get a physical because they did not want to lose me due to physical issues, even though I did not show any. During the physical, my doctor found that I have what she described as early type 2 diabetes. I was able to modify my lifestyle and keep my glucose levels and A1C in normal ranges by closely monitoring my diet. For more than five years, I had successfully done this to keep not only my doctor happy, but also to make sure I was able to stay around for my family as well.

Hypertension

High blood pressure, also referred to as hypertension, can be one of the major causes for a stroke. High blood pressure tends to damage and weaken arteries in such a way that they can lose flexibility. This loss of flexibility can cause arteries and blood vessels to ultimately burst or clog. Clogging causes blood clots to form more easily—no surprise there. While high blood pressure can damage all arteries throughout your body, weakened arteries in your brain are linked to a higher risk of stroke.

Cholesterol

The first time I personally became aware of the term *cholesterol* was in the mid 1990s. Cholesterol was getting a lot of publicity, and the medical community was rallying behind a movement that everyone should get screened for high cholesterol. If your cholesterol number was over 300, you should change your diet and talk to your doctor as soon as possible.

The company that I worked for even had local healthcare professionals come to our location and screen all six hundred employees for high cholesterol. My cholesterol was close to 300 at that time, so I made an attempt to lower it by modifying my diet.

Cholesterol itself is a soft, waxy fat found in the bloodstream and body's cells. Cholesterol fat is a lipid, and your body naturally produces all that it needs. Many foods that we eat can increase cholesterol levels. Cholesterol does not dissolve in blood and uses particles called lipoproteins to deliver it to our body's cells.

Over time, cholesterol values have been redefined, and acceptable cholesterol levels have been changed. Now there is LDL cholesterol and HDL cholesterol. The "LDL" and the "HDL" acronyms refer to low density lipoproteins and high density lipoproteins, respectively. LDL cholesterol is considered "bad" cholesterol as it carries cholesterol to the bloodstream and causes plaque build-up. Plaque build-up is a thick, hard substance that can clog arteries, over time possibly resulting in a stroke. HDL cholesterol is "good" cholesterol, with the HDL carrying cholesterol away from cells and to your liver to be filtered out of your bloodstream and removed from your body. Rule of thumb: Keep the LDL level low and the HDL levels relatively high.

You should have your cholesterol levels checked by your doctor. He or she can use various methods to change your cholesterol levels and thus reduce the risk of another stroke.

Smoking

Smoking is generally bad for your health and can cause lung cancer, heart problems, and lead to stroke. There are more than seven thousand different toxic chemicals in cigarette smoke. Many of these chemicals are transferred from your lungs to your bloodstream. I remember when I first started smoking, the first couple of puffs made me dizzy and disoriented. Almost fifty years later, after my stroke, I would get the same "rush" at times. This "rush" is due to some of the toxic chemicals entering my bloodstream.

Two major smoking-related factors are fluctuations in cholesterol and changes in blood vessel and artery walls. Smoking reduces the levels of HDL, or "good" cholesterol, and increases levels of LDL or "bad" cholesterol, both of which are covered in more detail earlier in this chapter.

The "rush" a person gets when he or she starts smoking can begin with the introduction of all of those toxic chemicals into the bloodstream. When those toxic chemicals build up, all kinds of bad things can happen to the blood vessel wall function and strength. Vessels work by flexion and contraction of the walls to move the blood along. Smoking causes the walls to harden and lose the flexibility; as a result, they can't move your blood as efficiently. Additionally, the build-up of fatty tissue can cause restrictions in arteries, often resulting in blood clotting. The blood clots can close or block arteries and deprive parts of the brain of oxygen and lead to stroke.

I guess for me, after smoking for forty-eight years, I am finally seeing these risks of smoking as being somewhat real, and I have decided to quit. My doctor was aware of my smoking both before and after my stroke, and she always talked about it with me every time I saw her. The last time I went to see her, she was thrilled to hear me finally ask for aids to stop smoking. I don't like to sound like a reformed smoker, but want to suggest that if you smoke, you should talk to somebody about stopping.

Watch Your Weight

Being overweight or having a very sedentary life style carry with them a higher risk of stroke. People who are excessively overweight (obese) generally are dealing with one or more of the factors discussed above. These concerns can include high glucose levels and, ultimately, diabetes; high blood pressure; and high fat and cholesterol levels. Obviously, the more overweight and/or less active you are, the bigger the risk that you have for a stroke. It is very important to consult your doctor for guidance with any weight problems.

All of the issues I listed have one thing in common. They all have less-than-desirable cells occupying the bloodstream. All these issues in the arteries or bloodstream can cause clotting in the brain. The clotting, if it builds up over time, can block the arteries or blood flow in part of the brain and lead to a loss of oxygen to part of the brain. The part of your brain subject to loss of oxygen causes cells to die off, resulting in a stroke.

Stress

If you have a lot of stress in your life, you are at a high risk for stroke. Unfortunately, there is relatively little information available as to how stress affects a person who has a stroke. In my case, prior to my stroke, my cholesterol was on the high side of standards but not excessively high. I have type 2 diabetes, but I kept my glucose levels well within acceptable levels, as well as my A1C levels (a measurement that concerns level of hemoglobin in the blood). I mentioned that I smoked and had for most of my life. I smoked about a pack of cigarettes a day, and showed no indications of heart or lung disease. I was quite active and always spent a fair amount of time getting strenuous exercise.

My attending ER physician pretty much attributed the cause of my stroke to stress, based on our ER interview and testing of my blood. All of the testing for items mentioned above came back with results below or just slightly above the desired maximum levels. Through a process of elimination, we narrowed down the most likely cause of my stroke to stress, especially when I told him how much I had been working in the previous months leading up to my stroke and how little time I had spent relaxing during that time.

Medications

While I was in the hospital, I was given thirteen different prescription drugs. At the time I was discharged, I was given seven prescriptions for medications that I needed to continue taking. I was given a "pharmacy monograph" for each drug halfway through my stay for the first thirteen medications, and then when I was released I was given seven more, each coinciding with one of the medications, as you might have guessed. The pharmacy monograph is a three- to five-page document that describes the generic version of the drug (if the hospital used generics) as well as the brand version of the drug.

The monograph also describes how to use the information it contains, any warnings for the medication, primary and secondary uses, how to use the medication, what potential side effects the medication might have, precautions, possible drug interactions, what to do if an overdose is suspected, a section with general notes, what to do for a missed dose, and storage of the drug. The monograph for Tylenol, for example, is three pages long and is one of the shortest. The first thing these sheets tell you is that they are a summary!

Below, I've listed all of the drugs by alphabetical order of the generic drug name. Some of the prescriptions at the hospital are slightly different than those I first used at home. I have them all listed for you, and have noted if they were from the hospital or at home.

Colace is a trade name for the drug **docusate**. I was given 100 mg capsules in the hospital as a stool softener to prevent constipation. Docusate increases the amount of water in your stools and makes stools softer and easier to pass.

Ecotrin EC is a brand name for **aspirin**. Aspirin has a ton of uses for reducing pain, but the reason most stroke survivors are told by their doctors to take it is that it works as a blood thinner in low doses and can help prevent blood clots. The dose I take is 81 mg, which is baby aspirin. I take the flavored chewable version to offset all of the drugs I have taken that can't be chewed.

Hydrochlorothiazide (HCTZ) 25 mg tablet. HCTZ is a diuretic or water pill that allows your body to make more urine to get rid of extra sodium and water. It is used to prevent strokes, heart attacks, and kidney issues by lowering your blood pressure. HCTZ can reduce swelling of your ankles and feet along with reducing shortness of breath.

Lioresal is a brand name for **baclofen**. Baclofen is prescribed to stroke survivors to treat muscle tightness or cramping and spasms. It is a muscle relaxant and as such reduces spasms, pain, and stiffness. By using this drug, you can do more daily activities and move around better. Baclofen is often started at a low dose and increased as needed. Once your doctor feels you can be taken off this drug, it is necessary to gradually reduce the dosage rather than stop at once. It can also be administered through a pump system.

Botox is a drug that is prescribed for many stroke survivors. It acts to reduce spasticity in affected arms, hands, and fingers. It is injected into the muscles (in low-dosage amounts) to relax them. I was not given Botox injections at all for spasticity. Muscle pain and spasticity were not a major issue with my recovery. Many times it is given to also reduce pain.

Lipitor is a brand name for **atorvastatin**. I was given 20 mg tablets of Lipitor when I was in the hospital. Along with eating correctly, Lipitor lowers bad cholesterol and fats in the bloodstream and raises good cholesterol. Lowering LDL and raising HDL helps prevent stroke and heart attacks.

Lopressor is a brand name for **metoprolol**. This is a drug that is used to treat high blood pressure, which is also known as hypertension. High blood pressure can lead to strokes, heart attacks, and kidney failure. This is another drug to be weaned off by using gradually lower doses instead of suddenly stopping at once.

Micro-K is a brand name for **potassium chloride**, and I took it in 10 mg tablets. Potassium is an important part of your blood. It's necessary so that your nerves, muscles, cells, heart, and kidneys can properly function. Potassium is normally controlled by diet, but to control it by diet you have to eat properly.

Miralax is a brand name for **polyethylene glycol** (PEG) 3350. This is a powdered form of a stool softener for treating occasional constipation. It's known as an osmotic type laxative that increases bowel movements. Miralax powder gets mixed with a liquid and is available over the counter. Once it is properly mixed, you drink it.

Nicoderm Transdermal Nicotine Patches. I mentioned earlier about how I smoked about a pack of cigarettes a day. While I was in the hospital, there were tons of restrictions about smoking. That and the idea that I was not able to get outside by myself pretty much made up my mind that it was time to quit smoking. Nicoderm is an over-the-counter drug that allows you to get the nicotine rush from smoking but gradually reduces the amount over time until you no longer crave nicotine.

Plavix is a brand name for **clopidogrel**. It works by blocking platelets from forming blood clots. It can leave you susceptible to easier bruising, but it does keep blood vessels open and prevents clotting.

Prinivil 20 mg tablets are a brand name for **lisinopril**. Prinivil is used to treat hypertension or high blood pressure. It is an ACE inhibitor and allows blood to flow more easily by relaxing blood vessel walls. It's intended to help prevent heart attacks, strokes, and kidney concerns.

Restoril 15 mg capsules are actually **temazepam**. Restoril is a sleeping medication that prevents insomnia. I found myself waking up after as little as an hour of sleep at night, which is why the nurse suggested trying the drug. After two or three nights, I didn't feel any change in my sleeping, so I decided to take them no longer.

Tylenol is a 325 mg tablet and a brand name for **acetaminophen**. Tylenol is used to reduce fever and treat moderate pain. It's been around long enough that I really doubt much more explanation is necessary.

These thirteen drugs were given to me at one time or another while I was in the hospital for twenty-eight days. You probably noted that there were multiple drugs that did the same thing. In those cases, the hospital folks were trying to find the best drugs for me as an individual. I was having blood drawn nearly every day to see which medications were best for me.

When I was discharged, I was given prescriptions for continuing the Lipitor, Lopressor, Nicoderm, Plavix, and Prinivil. I was also given a prescription for **glucophage** and for **Theragran M.**

The **Glucophage** was a 500 mg tablet for **metformin**. In the hospital I was given daily injections for Metformin. The doctors decided that tablets would be more convenient when I was discharged. Metformin is used to control high blood sugar in people who have type 2 diabetes. The final prescription was for **Theragram M** tablets, which are a **multivitamin**.

I still take atorvastatin, metoprolol, and lisinopril for my stroke. I also take Doxazosin, which is for controlling urination to allow me to sleep all night. My doctor has taken me off of Plavix and replaced it with daily baby aspirin, and, instead of Theragen M, I use an over-the-counter multivitamin. I also take a daily Allegra D for allergies.

I had never taken any drugs whatsoever before having my stroke. I still get excited each time my doctor tells me that I no longer need to take a particular medication. I really can't complain about having to take four prescription medications.

Many people are taking additional medications for depression and other reasons. In the case of stroke, this type of medication is often necessary and important. I am very fortunate that I do not have to take prescription drugs for such reasons.

There is one other thing I would like to say about prescription drugs. My sister-in-law had a heart and lung transplant a number of years ago. At one time she was taking more than fifty different medications a day. I truly feel blessed to be taking only four prescriptions and three over-the-counter meds a day.

I am now more than six years separated from my stroke, and periodically I remain amazed that I am still making progress with my recovery. I also realize that my recovery has not been and never will be over. I often think about the many people who consider my problems as very significant, when to me they are not at all burdensome.

Chapter 11

Attitude

WHEN I FIRST OUTLINED THIS BOOK, I CONSIDERED BREAKING THIS CHAPTER INTO TWO CHAPTERS. The first was going to be called "Negative Attitudes and Stroke" and the second "Positive Attitudes and Stroke." My thoughts were that the chapter about negative attitudes and stroke was going to be ten blank pages, with a chapter title on the first page and page numbers only on the next nine pages—otherwise, no text. The second of the two was going to be a cheerleading chapter telling you how to think only about being positive.

The further I researched stroke survivors, the more I found out that to just stick ten blank pages in here for negatives would be just plain wrong. While I have been in a position to be extremely positive in my outlook and recovery, there are a sizeable number of stroke survivors who are not.

In most cases of surviving a stroke, your or the person's life will be slightly different at best and perhaps a disaster at worst. I think it's safe to say that not one of the approximately eight hundred thousand people in the United States who suffer a stroke each year wake up one morning being excited that they were going to have a stroke that day. I know I certainly didn't. Even people with TIAs have the possibility of changes to their bodies that are unexpected. In my case, I walked into the hospital on a Friday morning under my own power and left my second hospital four weeks later in a wheelchair that I could hardly move by myself. For a guy who was as physically active as I was, that was a huge change. I lost the use of "only" my affected side and had a relatively minor change in my speech. I did not lose any of my cognitive abilities at all.

What if I had lost my cognitive abilities? What if I had developed aphasia, which is the inability to form thoughts into effective communication? What if I were not able to eventually walk again or able to live by myself again? What if I were not able to drive again or eventually interact in society again? Before my stroke, all of these activities were a basic part of my existence, as they are for most of us. To be unable to ultimately perform any of these would have been devastating. While I had a major stroke, I was "lucky" that it was not worse than it was. Not everyone who survives a stroke is as "lucky" in the long run as I was. I really have to say that most of my recovery came as a result of a lot of hard work on my part, as well as a very positive attitude.

In previous chapters I talked about my hospital stay, inpatient rehabilitation, and outpatient rehabilitation. I received very good care in this process and am very thankful for that care. Yet, what happens when the insurance money for rehabilitation runs out, and you are on your own with a big part of your body and possibly your thought process still not functioning? Worse than that, what if you are not married and live alone with no family nearby? What about the bills? What if you don't get the excellent care I received? There are a few of us who are very fortunate and can afford almost unlimited rehabilitation. There are many who can afford only little or no rehabilitation, and there are some, like me, who have relatively little rehabilitation before the insurance money runs out.

Unfortunately, there are no answers that I or anyone can provide that will guarantee you a favorable outcome in all of these situations. There are no "magic bullets" for recovery after you have been discharged from medical care.

Many of the stroke victims I have come in contact with over the past few years haven't had the care and therapy that I have had. Oftentimes, this is because they live in out-of-the-way locations, where strokes are an exceptional medical event. These people in many cases suffered TIAs and the doctors did what they could; from a medical standpoint, nothing else was needed. That is what they say about TIA. You have it for a very short time, and about half the time there is no evidence on an MRI or CT scan that they even occurred. In other cases, the patient might have been transported to other facilities hundreds of miles away; once discharged, they returned home where only minimum stroke rehabilitation therapy was available. Other people really don't know what happened, due to being in a coma, or they lost many of their cognitive abilities. The family was unsure of what questions to ask of the doctors, so neither the patient nor the family ultimately had any idea of what happened either mentally or physically when the stroke occurred.

It is important that the family member or whoever will provide care for the stroke survivor understands all of the ramifications of the stroke. That is not meant to suggest that whomever the stroke survivor lives with has to have a thorough understanding of every brain function; but they should at least attempt to gain a basic understanding of how the brain functions. If the stroke survivor has lost cognitive abilities, it is even more important that the caregiver and family members have at least a minimal understanding of the functions that were lost. If the caregiver doesn't have training in the medical arts, they should ask the doctors to simplify their comments—put them in laymen's terms, so to speak (pun intended)—so that they are to be understood in the simplest terms. Don't ever be afraid to ask the doctor to thoroughly explain what happened this way. This knowledge will be very important to understand what the stroke survivor is personally living with, but also in follow-up visits to doctors, as well as for things like applying for disability benefits and other financial assistance.

In chapter 1, I wrote that my first day in the hospital, I was thankful that God had given me what I thought was a very well-deserved vacation. Then the second day I started a new career, that being the best possible 'recovery' from my stroke. I shared these thoughts with my daughter, my neurologist, a couple of my therapists, and one other person, that being a counselor.

Counseling

The hospital I was in for my inpatient therapy had a staff psychiatrist. He was very intelligent and easy to talk to. We talked a little bit about my background and what my thoughts had been since having my stroke. I shared with him my thoughts about being on vacation as well as my new career. He was quite impressed with my thinking. He gave me a business card and told me that if I ever needed anything, to call him. As he finished up our visit, he also said that he expected me to do well and he doubted I would ever talk to him again. As much as I liked him and enjoyed his company, I never called him. I thought that his time could be better spent with other patients. I am sure it was.

I mentioned the psychiatrist because there are times when many people could and should have considered meeting with him. In my case, I never saw a need for his services. If you feel the need to talk to a psychiatrist, psychologist, or even a hospital ombudsman or any other counselor, and you have the resources available, you should do so. This type of professional service can really help when you're first trying to cope with a stroke. If this service is available to you, the best thing that you can do is to at least talk to that person and see what help they can offer. In many cases, they can make a huge difference in your recovery.

Family Involvement

If you are a family member of a stroke survivor, it is a really great idea to visit with the therapists or the doctor responsible for the therapy to get a decent understanding of what he or she is going through. In my case, I was assigned to a doctor who worked with a spine and rehab associates group that was ultimately responsible for my rehab. This doctor was a great resource for my daughter, and the three of us met several times. My daughter asked questions of the doctor until she could understand just what the doctor's goals and directions for the therapists were. It made the whole concept of the therapy that much easier for my daughter, and it made me feel far more comfortable that she had a better understanding.

Great Therapists Redux

I was involved with three types of inpatient therapy. These

were physical, occupational, and speech. My physical therapist was the oldest of the three and the most recent to complete her training. She was very pleasant to work with and at the same time pushed me the hardest of the three. She was the most fun to joke around with, and that might be why she felt comfortable enough to push me harder in my recovery. Although I didn't walk unassisted at all in the hospital, her pushing allowed me to walk with a cane very soon after my discharge from the hospital.

My inpatient occupational therapist was a very quiet young lady who had a somewhat weird work schedule in that she worked three days during the week and both weekend days. I would work with her twice during the week, and then with another lady on another day during the week. The second lady I worked with was fun as well. The thing about the primary occupational therapist was that she really was not fully booked up on the weekends, so whenever she had a chance she would come and get me on Saturdays and even one Sunday morning. We would go to a different therapy gym on another hospital floor and work on different things than what my therapy actually called for. She told me that this allowed her to try new things out to see how they worked. I know she didn't bill my insurance for these weekend sessions, and I really appreciated that. Her use of other therapies actually did some good, too.

My speech therapist was the youngest of the three inpatient therapists. She really acted the most professional of the three as well. As I said earlier, speech therapy is much more than just speaking. For my first two weeks there, she prepared a different breakfast in the hospital's therapy gym for up to eight of us. We ate at 9 A.M., after which she did most of the cleanup. She then held her sessions with who knows how many patients. The actual speech part of the therapy was agonizingly simple and boring. After my second week, I talked to her about my being very soft-spoken pre-stroke and promising her I would do my best to speak louder, which I have done. She also kept testing me for cognitive ability, and one day I showed her on my laptop how to set up a personal budget for her. After I demonstrated my cognitive ability to her, we had a much less stressful relationship. Her therapy sessions were much more fun for both of us, although they stopped soon after.

OK, I know what you're thinking—like I have done in a few other places in the book, you see me repeating myself, like in how I again bring up the three therapists. Admit it; you were questioning my cognition. Well, the reason I wrote this again was that I had great therapists worth bragging about a second time. My outpatient therapists were equally great. What I did, though, was to learn from each the manner by which they presented their respective specialties to me, the patient. I was able to use their methods to both of our advantages and get the most from them. I described my thoughts and their methods earlier and am not going to repeat what each did for me, other than to say that I really believe I got the best from each of my therapists for my situation. They provided me with the desire to keep working with my disabilities on my own, beyond their therapy, to continue to improve myself as well. This, to me, is just as important.

Another Stroke Survivor

A few years ago I met a stroke survivor and his wife at an event. They were in their late sixties. Our discussion got around to his therapy and recovery. The wife scoffed at her husband's therapists' abilities, saying that she knew she could have done much better with no training than his therapists had done. As far as she was concerned, they did nothing for him. From my perspective, he was doing pretty well. He was talking and walking, although he still used his cane. He did not have much use of his affected arm and hand but was only six months poststroke. From what they told me of how he was when he was in the hospital, it appeared to me that he was doing really well. I did not want to get into a discussion about his therapists with her, as in her mind she had lost her husband as she knew him. She needed someone to "blame" for this, and his therapists were the unlucky scapegoats. Therapy is a two-way street. You will get much more out of it when you contribute as much to it as possible.

I want to bring this couple into this book to lead the discussion in several directions at once. She really did not understand the effects of the stroke on her husband's life.

I suspect that his doctor might not have made sure that this couple was made aware of the long-term effects of his having had a stroke. Many people have contact with heart patients who have heart attacks or bypass surgery and recover in weeks or months at the most. Even heart transplants have become so commonplace with recovery taking place in a few months. Yet, here they were with a stroke survivor who was recovering very quickly from a stroke; in her case, at least, it was not quick enough. I kind of felt sorry for him that his wife really didn't understand all of what he was going through, but he seemed to be happy with his recovery so far.

Hard to Understand

It is very hard to relate to stroke recovery for several reasons. Less than one-fourth of 1 percent of the population of the United States have a stroke in a given year. That is a very small number. That relates to about one person out of four hundred. Take out those who die from a stroke, the number of people who have multiple strokes, and the number of people who have TIAs or ministrokes, and the number of people who have had massive strokes becomes more like one in a thousand or more people. Most of us don't even know a thousand people very closely so the exposure we get to a massive stroke survivor is almost nonexistent. Many of us who have had massive strokes have a very hard time with our mobility; therefore, we are restricted to staying home, or at best getting out in the world on a very limited basis, further reducing everyone else's exposure to stroke survivors.

Prior to having my massive stroke at age sixty-one, I had not had exposure to more than three or four stroke survivors (that I know of) in my entire life. Over those sixty-one years, I had met and interfaced with, literally, tens of thousands of people. I was also a trained medical first responder for a volunteer fire department. I had never gotten a call for someone having a stroke. For these reasons, I didn't know what was happening to me during my stroke, nor did I know what would happen afterward. My doctor, my neurologist, and a nurse all explained to my daughter and me what my therapy would consist of.

My point in all this is that we, as a society, do not really have a thorough understanding of how stroke changes people and how to handle those changes. This pertains to not only stroke survivors, but also to family and many caregivers. I know, for example, that my daughter, at times, didn't realize that some of the snacks I wanted to eat were not going to kill me. In her mind I was a diabetic and, therefore, just plain could not eat anything with sugar in it. Nearly every food that we eat has natural sugars in it. What I learned over the years was which foods have excessive sugars and how to control my sugar levels by not eating large portions of most foods. My blood sugar and A1C numbers were well within the limits my doctor set for me, but Tami and I did have several "discussions" while I stayed with her about snacks that were acceptable. I still do everything to control my diabetes, and my doctor is happy with my A1C and blood sugar levels.

Knowledge is Power

I have gone way overboard in my desire to learn about people with strokes, but that is my nature at almost everything I do. If you have had a stroke, or are caring for someone who has, I suggest you do a bit of research on the Internet as well as *ask your doctor* any questions you might have. Be aware that the Internet is not always the place from which to get 100 percent accurate information. Also keep in mind that every stroke is different, so what you might find on the Internet might not apply to a specific person, but learning general information is pretty good on the Internet.

It is possible to gather basic knowledge of the stroke that you or a family member has had without being a doctor. That will help when something comes along that might or might not be related to the stroke. I am very fortunate to have a very good doctor; my Medicare supplement plan encourages visits every three months. I ask her one or two questions every time I visit her. One time my daughter had taken a photo of the two of us shortly before our appointment. In this photo it was somewhat apparent that my affected leg did not appear the same as my unaffected leg. I asked her about this. She reminded me that I had had the stroke and that it was OK if there was a difference in appearance. Most of what I have asked her is similar. My concerns are due to the stroke or to my age, but it is good to know that. In other cases she has suggested I take nonprescription drugs, and this has been helpful. I now take a daily multiple vitamin and a daily allergy pill, and I don't mind taking them. Both of these helped me very much. At times she has also stopped medications as well.

When you have a doctor's appointment, it is often a good thing to prepare for it in advance. The most important thing to do before the visit is to have a list of questions that you want answers to. If your doctor has scheduled an appointment with you for a stroke follow-up, he or she will generally go over a routine set of issues to cover and ask questions that fall into that routine. Because every stroke is different, you might have questions that are specific to you that do not fall into the routine. After your doctor has done his or her routine exam, it is your turn to ask questions. Do not ever be intimidated by your doctor, and don't be afraid to have him or her take more time with you. They are there to perform the steps needed to improve your health. They cannot answer your questions if you never ask them. They might be like my doctor and tell you that your question is normal for you and not to worry, but they might also find your concern to be important enough for more diagnosis. Either way, you will know more, and the experience will be far more positive for both of you.

A Friend in Stroke Recovery

I have a friend who is living in a nursing home to recover from her stroke. She was four months poststroke and was happy with the care and rehab she was getting there. She was in her late thirties, had not lost any cognitive abilities, and was truly excited with her recovery to date. She would ask me questions about rehabilitation and I would answer her if I could. One day I asked her what kind of stroke she had and what area of her brain was affected. She was unaware of whether she had had an ischemic or hemorrhagic stroke. Apparently, her physicians never told her. She has since found out that she had an ischemic stroke, which can be very valuable knowledge should she have to visit an emergency room or doctor when she travels. She is a very positive person and has since begun asking her doctors and nurses more questions about her stroke.

A long time ago, when I was in college, I once took a psychology class. One thing that I remember from that class was a lesson where we learned that knowledge is power. Now, some people never share their knowledge; however, I always did in my career, and I believe my employees and others had a lot of respect for me because of my willingness to share. We learned that having knowledge empowers us to handle any situation, and that would obviously include recovery from a stroke. I know that the more I learn about my stroke, the more comfortable I feel. In my past life, I always told people that the only dumb question was the one that never got asked. This is truer now than I ever realized before.

I would guess that by now about half of the people reading this are thinking that I am making all this stuff up about my being positive about this all the time. I have to admit that I have felt funny about my stroke a couple of times. My early walking pace was excruciatingly slow (it's far better now, but still very slow). Any time I would walk with someone, they would usually walk at their normal pace. This in turn would leave me way back in their dust. It would make me feel like I was left out. I'm sure that the friends or family members I was walking with didn't even realize how I felt. One day when I had just resumed driving poststroke, I went to a grocery store to buy a book. There was a cashier that had no customers in line, so I headed for that cashier. I was no more than fifteen feet away and a young lady with a cart full of groceries beat me to the cashier. I just got in line behind her and glared at that lady. After she looked at me three or four times, she could no longer look at me.

These experiences were frustrating to say the least. However, I took these experiences as incentives to recover more quickly and fully. Many people would take situations like this and get angry with themselves for being "different." Many would want to hide at home and not be among "normal" people. There is a basic fear of this in most people. I simply do not let these differences from normal get me down. In fact, I often embrace these changes and let them guide my "new" normal.

Cognitive abilities range from people like me, who have literally lost none, to people who have lost a large part of their memory and thought processes. There are also people who develop aphasia, or, as you might remember, the lack of ability to communicate. Many people lose their thought "filters," and just plain say what they think all the time. Stroke victims who lose their "filters" might often seem insulting or quick-tempered. These people might want something "now" and get upset if it takes even a few minutes to get it. They really don't mean any harm. The best way to deal with them is to quietly ask them to be patient. They will often outgrow this behavior.

Years ago I remember reading a comparison of successful people versus unsuccessful people. The chart below tells some of the differences and is very appropriate for stroke survivors:

Successful people: Continuously learn or try new things
Unsuccessful people: Think they know it all so don't try new things

Successful people: Talk about ideas or concepts
Unsuccessful people: Talk about or degrade other people

Successful people: Take responsibility for failures
Unsuccessful people: Blame others for their failures

Successful people: Forgive others
Unsuccessful people: Hold a grudge

Successful people: Embrace change
Unsuccessful people: Afraid of change

Successful people: Want others to succeed
Unsuccessful people: Want others to fail
Successful people: Embrace a new situation and work on improving it or curing it
Unsuccessful people: Are afraid of new situations and will not work on improving or curing it

I always strived to be successful pre-stroke and continue to do so. I added the last lines of the chart specifically for stroke survivors. *Do not be afraid of a new situation due to your stroke but rather work on improving or curing it.*

I am very fortunate to live in a community where the people are generally very well-educated and intelligent overall. The people of this community embraced me post-stroke, and this support has encouraged me. I don't feel uncomfortable in any shopping environment or in any restaurants. Not all communities are like mine. In some cases a stroke survivor and his or her family might want to be selective in where to shop or eat out.

Seek Out Others

I recommend that stroke survivors seek others in their communities where they can receive the encouragement to support them. Groups can include stroke support groups, church groups, various volunteer groups in hospitals, VFW, Shriners, or similar groups. Most often these groups will welcome stroke survivors who can help with the organization's goals in some small way. These groups can give stroke survivors a reason to get out and mingle with others. Even if the groups meet only once a week or once a month, it all helps in your overall recovery.

Helping a New Friend

One day after I returned to my apartment poststroke, I was sitting out on my patio on a nice summer afternoon enjoying myself and the weather. An older, retired lady was walking her dog and stopped to introduce herself. While chatting, she told me that she didn't have a car, so she very seldom left the apartment complex. I asked her what she did for shopping, and she said that another lady would stop at the store for her when she needed anything. I told her that I went grocery shopping every Wednesday morning to take advantage of the senior discount and offered to take her with me. She got pretty excited about this and for the last four years we have gone shopping together nearly every Wednesday. The two or three hours a week is important to her and gives her a sense of independence, so I will keep taking her. These kinds of things not only help others, but can help you as well.

I set my routine to include laundry and housecleaning on Mondays and Tuesdays. I would be pretty much fatigued at first and needed most of the two days for these chores. Eventually a friend of mine and I started to have a set lunch appointment every Tuesday. It worked out really well as I became less fatigued and was able to do my chores in much less time. Now, I had something planned every Tuesday and Wednesday.

Near the end of my second summer poststroke, I was able to get out a couple of times a week in addition to my Tuesday lunches, such as to take part in the aphasia training at a local university and in joining the local Rotary club. One Friday afternoon, as I mentioned earlier, I went to get a cheeseburger at an upscale burger joint. I had not been to this place in years, but for some unknown reason wanted to go there that Friday. As I was leaving, there was a gentleman coming in who obviously was a stroke survivor. He was holding his affected arm just as I was, and walked with a cane. We exchanged phone numbers, and I agreed to call him the next week.

There was also that time I met this man and his wife the next Friday for dinner. He showed me some materials from a program he was involved in for aphasia training of graduate students in speech pathology at a local major university. He asked me to join him the following Thursday. I was welcomed into this group and that took care of my Thursdays for eight to ten weeks a semester for two or three semesters every year. I don't have aphasia, but do all I can to help those who do to communicate with the students and vice versa. Later, I talked to the program manager and found out she really didn't know that I was invited, but she is grateful that I am there to help her somewhat.

During my fourth year poststroke, I went to a charitable event at a large private automobile collection in town. While there, I ran across a lady that I knew well when I was in the local Chamber of Commerce. She was there as part of the local Rotary Club that was affiliated with the charity that was benefiting from the event. Eventually, she started introducing me to other Rotarians and talking about my joining the Rotary Club. I met her at her office a few days later for more information, and eventually joined the Rotary Club. In some ways it was like coming home again, as many Rotary members are also members of the Chamber of Commerce. Members of our Rotary include all professions in the community from business people and owners to lawyers and doctors to many local government officials including our Congressperson. Everyone there is very supportive to me as well, and I hope I can make a contribution to our community and the club. Rotary meets for breakfast on Wednesday mornings, so that works well with the timing of my weekly shopping trips.

When I turned sixty-six, I visited our senior citizens center. I wanted to see if they had anything I would be interested in. I have since joined it, mostly for the chance to associate with fellow seniors and eat lunch on Mondays. I have been involved with their annual family fun fest and have attended a political forum there as well.

I have limited use of my affected (right) leg and even more limited use of my affected (right) arm and hand, but I have not let that stop me from keeping myself busy and active. I certainly don't do any of this stuff for income but rather volunteer for all these activities. Being this active gives me a sense of belonging and usefulness poststroke. In addition, these activities give me the incentive to continue my recovery. I personally attribute any speech improvements to the speech pathology program, and I have been walking without my cane more as well as climbing steps much better the last year as a result of my activities.

I really don't want to say that if I can do these activities, anyone can. I know that every stroke survivor will not be able to be as active as I am every week. Fatigue is a problem for many stroke survivors, but doing a little cleaning every day can make a difference with your sense of accomplishment. Simple things like cooking and baking will also give you a sense of accomplishment. I usually bake a cake or brownies or cookies at least once every two weeks. I would also recommend that every stroke survivor spend a few hours a week doing some form of activity out of the house, if you are able. If you are in a care facility, ask if you can volunteer to help out in that facility. Even just getting out of the room to socialize with other residents will help. Being as active as possible will make a difference in your life and in your recovery from your stroke.

Chapter 12

Survivors I Know

OVER THE LAST FOUR YEARS, I HAVE HAD THE GOOD FORTUNE TO MEET SEVERAL STROKE SURVIVORS WITH VERY POSITIVE ATTITUDES, AND A COUPLE OF OTHERS WHO WERE NOT AS POSITIVE. These people range from truck drivers to carpenters to former business owners to dentists. The seven I chose for this chapter are people I met in town in various settings. Obviously, the names are not real but the descriptions are.

When I first met 'Don,' he was a man in his late fifties and was six years poststroke. Don was in the army in his youth and was getting all of his medical treatment at the local Veterans Administration hospital. He had relocated just a few months earlier to Tennessee from Florida. When he left the army, he went to college under the G.I. Bill for a while. After he dropped out, he went to work for a subcontractor for a builder in Florida. He claimed he eventually started his own subcontractor business as a framer, with twenty people working for him. This framing included interior walls and roofing. He had his stroke while on a jobsite, and, as a result of it, he had fallen and hit his head. He moved in with a sister after leaving the hospital, and sold his truck and tools. He overstayed his welcome with his sister and her family as he was very demanding. His sister made arrangements with his niece, who lived in my area, to move into an apartment that was at the other end of my building.

I met Don through his other sister from Florida; she moved in with him to become his caregiver. She had been in Tennessee for about three weeks when I moved back to my apartment. Unfortunately, she did not have a vehicle either, so she walked to the bank to cash his checks for cigarettes and groceries. Eventually, she talked Don into getting a few things for his apartment, including a vacuum cleaner among other things.

I agreed one morning to take Don and his sister to the nearest mass merchant, or what some people call a big-box store. This was the first I had seen Don walk outside of his apartment, and he could walk far better than I could at the time. We made the purchases and went back to the apartment. On the way back, he asked how he and his sister were going to assemble the vacuum. I offered to loan him the tools he needed, but he said with his bad arm there was no way he could do the assembly, and neither could his sister. I offered to try. I spent the next hour and a half sitting by myself on the patio and putting the vacuum together. When I was done, I put the packaging material into the box, told them it was done, and headed home with my tools.

Don refused to do anything in the apartment other than sit on the couch smoking and watching television all day. His sister literally did everything for him, including getting him glasses of water and cups of coffee during the day. A few days later, he asked if I would take him to the V.A. hospital for an appointment that he had made two weeks earlier for the next day. I got up early and got ready to get him there, but when I got to his apartment, he told me he didn't want to go and had canceled the appointment. A short time later, a lady he knew from Florida moved up and in with him, and his sister went back to Florida. This lady was twelve years older than he was and cherished her role as his caregiver, even though he was physically able to be her caregiver, if need be.

A few months later, Don and his live-in companion moved out. By that time, I was no longer talking to them much. He treated her like he was the victim, and she should be happy that he chose her to be with him. From what I saw over the three months or so that he was in my apartment complex was that he did not want anybody to realize he was much better. He was going to take advantage of his stroke for all it was worth. Don had told his sister that he was afraid to go out and have anyone see him fall again. Don was a very intelligent man who was easy to talk to, and it didn't appear as if he had lost any of his cognitive ability. I presumed that Don had had something of a negative attitude even before his stroke, and I really did not want his negative attitude affecting my recovery.

'Greg'

As I said earlier, I had started to go out more. One of the restaurants I frequented had a server I got to know pretty well. She contacted me one day and told me her ex-husband Greg had had a stroke a few days before and was now in a hospital in Texas. She wanted to know what to expect. Her daughter lived behind her on the next street over. Greg, my server friend's ex, was an over-the-road (long-distance) truck driver who basically lived in his truck but used his daughter's house as his permanent address, even though he was there only one or two days a month. While he was in the hospital, the company from which he leased his truck took it back and left his personal possessions that were in it with him in the hospital. She and her daughter were going to go get him from the hospital and bring him back to Tennessee. Since he had no insurance, the hospital in Dallas he had been admitted to did not start any rehabilitation program for him, and they left him with a gait belt and a hemi walker at his discharge. My waitress friend and her daughter had driven back home with everything he owned in the trunk, and with him in the back seat.

In the two years since moving back in with his daughter, Greg has gotten better with his recovery. He can walk with his hemi walker but he seldom leaves the house and has seldom been in public. He will get out in the yard at times but limits himself. I have offered to visit with him several times and to take him places nearby, but every time I have asked, he has declined. Given what I know of his life, I can maybe see why. He is in his mid-fifties and was pretty much a loner with no real home at the time of his stroke. I suggested to Greg's ex-wife that she should encourage her daughter to help him apply for Social Security and our state's Medicaid program. However, when I followed up with her, she was never sure if the two of them had or not. She did tell me once that he was never willing to go see any local doctors. Greg was also taking a chance on not having any insurance, and, therefore, had no access to any therapy. Yet he is alive and spends more time with his daughter and grandchildren than he was able to prestroke.

'Chuck'

When I had first started to get back to going out after returning to my apartment, I started to go back to our local Cruise-In car show on Friday evenings. It was there that I had the good fortune of meeting Chuck, who had had a stroke and was back at work. He was several years post-stroke and was employed at a local assembly plant for aircraft parts. He had partial use of his arm and leg on his affected side, and was working performing light-duty jobs.

Social Security had set his disability at 50 percent, so he was not getting his full disability, and his union had worked out his light duty at work on his behalf. He had very good insurance, which covered nearly all of his expenses. His only problem poststroke is prescription-drug coverage. He was taking more than ten prescription drugs for which he was paying a large amount of his income. Unlike me, he was able to keep his car and was still showing it. In addition, he was able to drive long distances to visit his family out of state while on vacations. Every night at the Cruise-In, he talked about his recovery and what he was doing at work. His attitude was always very positive, and he was great to talk to. He was not going to let his stroke affect his life.

'Richard'

Another gentleman, Richard, also was a regular at the Cruise-In. Richard was an elderly man, a semi-retired dentist. Richard was in his early seventies, and was a fit man who was six-foot-six. His son was an inch taller and they both were very professional in their manner and attitude. Richard kept his practice open part-time to care for his long-time patients, especially some who had limited ability to pay for dental work elsewhere. Richard had a TIA last winter and was hospitalized for a week. He was given a therapy routine to follow, and, believe it or not, he resumed his part-time practice two weeks later. His biggest disability was a loss of balance, which necessitated his use of a cane. At the end of the summer, Richard was still showing his Mustang each week and was using his cane. The car was always clean, and he took it to a few other shows during the summer. While Richard doesn't have the same energy level he has had in the past, he is certain that is due more to an age factor than an effect of his stroke. This man amazes me for sure. Richard is a true inspiration to all stroke survivors.

'Roger'

I met Roger and his wife at the grocery store one Wednesday morning when they were doing their weekly shopping on senior day. I found out that he had had his stroke a few years earlier and had recovered fairly well. Roger spoke very clearly and walked with a cane very well, but he had little use of his right arm and hand. Roger was driving, and he and his wife would see their out-of-town children several times a year. Unfortunately, he didn't want to talk about his stroke, so we didn't. I did find out that he had owned his own successful business before he had his stroke. Roger blamed his stroke for a significant change in his life. He was forced to sell his business after his stroke, and that was about five years earlier than he had once anticipated. The stroke had also changed his retirement plans as well. He and his wife were always interesting to talk to, and I would see them almost every week at the grocery store. Unfortunately, Roger also was fighting lung cancer and I seldom see him anymore, but I often see his wife and she reports he is doing as well as can be expected.

'Jim'

Jim is my favorite stroke survivor. He is mentioned elsewhere in this book. Jim had his brain stem stroke about fifteen years ago in another state. He was at that time diagnosed as having multiple sclerosis. His wife was offered a job transfer to the Nashville area about six years ago, and they moved here to be closer to family. As a result of the move, Jim's wife made an appointment with a doctor here who wanted to do a follow-up MRI to determine if there were any changes in his MS. After reading the MRI, Jim's doctor determined that he had had a brain stem stroke and didn't have MS—not at all. The stroke had affected his right side, and he also had aphasia, which, as you know, is a brain deficiency that affects a person's ability to communicate with others. I will discuss aphasia in Chapter 13.

Jim had been married to his wife for many years pre-stroke. She stood beside him through the MS diagnosis, and they are still together. Jim had a great career as a teacher and was a guidance counselor in a high school when he had his stroke. He was now capable of driving again and in fact had spent a couple of years driving a small bus for an organization that shuttled people with disabilities locally a couple of days a week. After he stopped driving the van, he went on to volunteer for a hospital three days a week delivering mail. I met Jim as I was leaving a restaurant while he was walking in. We exchanged phone numbers, and I called him the next week. As I mentioned earlier in the book, Jim is the one who got me to start attending an aphasia group he was attending at a local university.

Jim drove me to the university that first time, and we sat in the lunch room at the rehab center. As more aphasia survivors came in, I was introduced to them and we had a nice chat. A bit later a group of post-grad students came in with their clinical manager. Bill introduced me to the new group and the manager. She (the manager) set me up with a student and one of the aphasia members to go to a computer area and work on a current events PowerPoint slide for later in the day. We moved to another area, where the manager gave me an iPad on which to play games while the students worked with the other people until lunchtime. After lunch, we all presented our current events slides, did our book club review, and met in what was called our "big group activity."

Jim and I became pretty good friends. Communication was difficult, but by asking him questions as simply as I could, it was possible to get simple answers from him. When traffic was light on the way to the aphasia group, or when it was my turn to drive, I would encourage Jim to come up with a "word of the day." These would often come from roadside billboards or even off semi-trucks, but he could come up with brief descriptions of the words he chose. When he came up with his words of the day and meanings, I could hear the excitement in his voice.

We made a couple of day trips as well. There is a small city nearby that is named the same as Jim's last name. This was our first day trip. We ate at a BBQ place there and drove around the downtown area. We continued a bit farther to the next city, where we saw a dam and the lake above the dam. We stopped in at the visitors' center for about a half-hour, and Jim looked at the exhibits and took a map of the lake with him.

The second day trip was to a museum nearby that was known for its antique tractors as well as antique farm machinery. A really neat display was a large collection of antique gas-powered laundry equipment, most of which had wooden tubs. Jim and I were both very impressed with this collection. There were some tractors made by the company that my high school was named after, and there was a tractor named the same as his last name with the same spelling. That generated some excitement on his part, and I even took a picture of Jim standing by that tractor. I printed that and gave it to Jim a few days later. We would also take back routes home from the university from time to time so he could see different scenery as well. I know Jim enjoyed our time together and know that I did as well.

'George'

I went into a restaurant one day and the hostess came to my table and started talking about her husband, George, who had had a stroke. I got his phone number and called him a few days later. George had met his wife when he worked in Louisiana. They decided to move to Tennessee, where they bought a rural property on which to eventually retire and build a nice log cabin. She worked as a hostess and he had a contract with the power company to keep the right of way for the high-tension lines bushhogged. His stroke came one afternoon when he was done for the day and had just finished loading his tractor onto his trailer. He couldn't move his right arm or leg. He was able to call first responders, who took him to the hospital.

George spent a few weeks in the hospital, and a neighbor picked up his truck and tractor for him. When he got out of the hospital, George sold his mowing equipment, and he and his wife decided to sell their property and move to her hometown in Canada. He had recovered well, was able to walk well, and was able to get up and down stairs surprisingly well. Three weeks after I met George, he and his wife were going to make the move. They were looking forward to retirement and gardening. They were a wonderful couple and very happy that he was able to recover as well as he did.

I chose these people to discuss here because they represent a good cross-section of stroke survivors that I met. Most are in their late fifties to seventies, but I was able to mention a thirty-year old here as well. Most of these people had been through at least some degree of rehabilitation. Most were able to live a decent-to-great life after their stroke, but not all were. The thing that impressed me the most about these people is that they are not afraid of what "normal" people might think, and they just go about their new lives as best they can.

The people I wrote about might or might not be typical of all stroke survivors. I realize that stroke survivors who don't get out in public often chose not to for various reasons; many become totally immobilized because of the severity and location of their brain injury. I was not able to meet any of those stroke survivors. That's why I was not able to get a true cross-section of people who have had strokes. I was also not able to come across many women stroke survivors about whom to get information, so this sample group does not fully represent all stroke survivors equally.

Since I had my stroke, I have met dozens of other survivors. I was able to get to know some of them fairly well, but I had just enough time with most of them for us to both acknowledge that we went through similar experiences. Most were easy to talk to about their stroke and even seemed somewhat excited to talk to someone else who had similar experiences. I tend to encourage social interaction among other stroke survivors, as the interaction can be quite rewarding.

There are a multitude of venues or organizations convenient for meeting other stroke survivors. One obvious way to meet others is to attend local stroke support groups. These support groups are available in many cities. If one is available in your area, I very much encourage you to visit at least a couple of times before deciding if it is or isn't right for you.

I have met several stroke survivors when I was out shopping at grocery stores and mass merchants. These meetings might be brief, but they can result in phone number exchanges leading to further contact. Restaurants are another place to make contacts, but these are usually more for an intimate situation. I have met stroke survivors at flea markets and car shows. I would imagine that home shows, boat shows, even county fairs might be good places to meet others. High school sporting events and other events such as softball and soccer might also have stroke survivors in attendance watching their children and grandchildren participate. The point is that it is possible to get out and enjoy such events. Not only will these be enjoyable for you, but you might make the acquaintance of others with similar experiences.

Another place to find support for both stroke survivors as well as caregivers is on social media such as Facebook. I follow a couple of groups on Facebook and have learned a lot from my fellow survivors there. Social media not only provides contact with those who get out in public, but also those who are homebound as well, and for caregivers who might provide insights into how their loved ones feel. These sites have group members in all stages of recovery from a few weeks out to many years out. Many people on these sites offer support and encouragement by relating their own personal experiences as well.

Chapter 13

A Few Words about Aphasia

THROUGHOUT MY LIFE I HAVE HAD OPPORTUNITIES TO TAKE ON QUITE A FEW LARGE PROJECTS. Some of these projects were work-related, but many were also personal projects. Most of these projects are done to learn and reach a definite goal. One of my more recent projects has been to learn something about aphasia. About 40 percent of stroke survivors end up with a form of aphasia. It also can affect people with massive brain injuries who are not stroke survivors. Quick review from earlier mentions: aphasia affects parts of the brain that control communication and the areas of speech, language understanding, reading, writing, and math.

When I was discharged from my first hospital and transferred to my second for rehabilitation, I was given a nicely printed twenty-eight-page "Stroke Booklet" that was intended to be "discharge education for patients and families." This booklet was quite detailed in most aspects of stroke, but was somewhat vague on aphasia. It devoted about a quarter-page to aphasia. It's a disability that certainly could use more exposure to make people aware of what it is and how to interact with people with aphasia.

As I mentioned earlier, my real exposure to aphasia came in my second year of recovery when I was walking out of a restaurant and another stroke survivor was walking in. He's the one who actually told me about and led me to an aphasia group that met at a local university, as I mentioned. So my exposure to aphasia and its significance to stroke survivors were pretty much accidental yet fortuitous.

Depending on where in the brain the damage occurred, aphasia might be severe enough to make communication all but impossible. On the other hand, it might be extremely mild or someplace in the middle. Following are several basic aphasia types for which I did some research and offer some insights:

A person with **Global aphasia** has what is considered to be the most severe form of aphasia. People with global aphasia will not be able to understand any spoken language or say more than a few simple words. In addition, these people cannot read or write.

Broca's aphasia is often times called "**nonfluent aphasia.**" People so affected might have severely reduced speech, able only to utter a few words. Someone with

Broca's aphasia will have a limited access to vocabulary, and speech can seem labored and clumsy. Broca's aphasia survivors will usually be able to understand speech and to read fairly well, but writing is often difficult.

Mixed NonFluent aphasia people have speech that takes more effort. It is a form of aphasia rarer than Broca's aphasia. Reading and writing are usually not above an elementary level; speech comprehension is low as well.

People with **Wernicke's aphasia** can relatively easily produce connected speech, but they will have a hard time understanding spoken words. This is also referred to as "**fluent aphasia**." Speech is still quite abnormal with sentence structure not hanging together and excessive use of irrelevant words. Reading and writing often are quite impaired as well.

Anomic aphasia is when people have a hard time deciding which words to use for a specific item. This is especially true in the use of verbs or nouns. If you have anomic aphasia, you will often feel frustration when searching for the right words, both in speaking and writing. You should not have a problem reading or understanding the speech of others.

Primary progressive aphasia is normally unrelated to stroke but is a symptom of a degenerative disease, such as Alzheimer's. Early phases of PPA will affect speech and language, and it will ultimately lead to other issues such as memory loss.

Just like every stroke is different, there is quite a bit of difference in aphasia types or combinations of aphasia. You may be able to speak fairly well, but not know your basic alphabet and have reading and writing problems. You may be able to do math just as you did in the past, or you may lose some or most of your capability for math or numbers. Your reading and writing comprehension may not be affected but your speech may be greatly affected. The aphasia effects you have will be dependent on what part of your brain is damaged.

A lot of the material written about aphasia compares having aphasia to living in a foreign country where you cannot understand the speech of anybody or cannot read the language and, therefore, cannot write anything that makes sense. Yet, you know in your own language what everything is or means. With aphasia you may not be able to name photos of basic utensils, even though you very well know what they are and what they do. Talk about a weird feeling to live with, but this is the type of life you may live with aphasia.

I belong to a unique aphasia group in Nashville. Our aphasia group has pretty much the same people in it year after year. The total number of people varies some, but it's safe to say it is in the sixteen-to-twenty range. We typically have a forty-year age difference between the "kids" and old people. The group tends to be more male than female, but I don't think that reflects the gender ratio of stroke survivors throughout the country.

Typically we have eight to ten students in the group.

The students are all college graduate students learning speech pathology. Usually the students are all female with one or two males thrown into the mix in a given year. These "kids" are very smart and tend to come from all over the US and, occasionally, other countries. This is not a typical support group that meets an hour a month, but rather more of a rehab group that meets once a week when school is in session. Our program starts at 9:30 in the morning and ends at 4:30 in the afternoon on Thursdays.

Our morning begins with a half-hour meet and greet, in which we all get up to date with what happened during the past week. At 10 A.M. we break into smaller groups and create PowerPoint slides of current event topics. At 11 we will continue work on current events or jointly work on group projects such as the topic of the day. Lunch is at noon, and at 12:30 we have a half-hour trivia contest.

At 1 P.M. we present our current-events slides, and at 2:00 we discuss the week's assigned reading in book club. Our fearless leader picks out a book to read in book club each semester. These books are easy to read and are books that I seldom would read, so this has allowed me to broaden my horizons. Our last three books have been based in Africa; they have been very entertaining as well as educational. Book club books are available as printed books, more or less a Cliffs Notes version for some, or as a "books on tape" version for some books. All of these events are conducted in several small groups where the survivors are grouped by ability.

After book club and a break, we go into what we call our big group. During the hour and fifteen minutes of big group, we try to cover three things. Big group generally starts out with a discussion of the word of the day, followed by group members taking their turns to discuss a favorite item of interest to them, and it winds up with a formal presentation of a general topic by one of the students.

It has been a lot of fun to be involved with this group. The students are all hard workers who try their best to work with each of us, and they are usually quite successful. The long-term aphasia survivors in the group have generally made some progress in the three years that I have been in this group, but the progress is not significant enough to be able to say that anyone has been 100 percent cured of aphasia. I really think such cures are very rare.

I just cannot say enough about how fortunate I feel to be involved with this great group of people.

Chapter 14

Personal Activities and Relationships

A S I MENTIONED EARLIER, MY STROKE OCCURRED IN DE-CEMBER 2011, AND I AM WRITING THIS CHAPTER IN JULY 2018. I have been working on this book off and on for some four years. Since having my stroke, I have been very fortunate to have had some incredible experiences. Now, when I say, "incredible experiences," I have to qualify that somewhat.

First of all, I am still recovering from a major stroke. I figure that I will continue to be in a state of recovery from my stroke as long as I am alive. In addition, my finances are in no way in the upper stratosphere. I live on a very small pension that supplements my Social Security. My age has moved my Social Security from Social Security Disability Insurance to Retirement; however, the

Social Security payments and Medicare coverage haven't changed. Keeping those restrictions in mind, my life is still incredible, and I look forward to getting up every day. Following are some of the life's highlights since my stroke.

I have the good fortune of having a Medicare Supplement Plan that emphasizes preventive care. That's why I see my primary-care physician four times a year. This spring, she told me that I was in excellent condition and that all I should do was keep on doing what I had been doing as far as maintaining my health. I reminded her that I had trouble walking and using my right arm and hand. She told me, even taking that into consideration, that I was still extremely healthy for a sixty-seven-year-old man. That made me feel really good about what I am doing.

I still attend the local stroke support group at the hospital where I had my inpatient therapy. The long-term survivors there give me a sense of success from my efforts, as I'm sure they get the same sense from mine. Even more important, though, is to show those patients in the hospital that there is the possibility of a good life after their strokes. I will keep going there as long as I am physically able to.

I also still attend the aphasia group at the major university. The core group of aphasia survivors has been there for years, and I've made many great friendships. Each semester we get one or two new people in the group, although, unfortunately, some drop out as well.

I've had the good fortune to be able to travel to and visit my oldest daughter twice, once in Dallas, Texas, and again in Daytona Beach, Florida. As much as I used to travel in the past, I have to admit I was somewhat apprehensive about traveling again. My apprehension was due to getting around in the airport terminals with my limited mobility more than anything. But airlines and terminal personnel have been very helpful, as I described earlier, and, overall, it is actually far easier for me to fly now than it was for the thousands of times I flew pre-stroke. In addition to the joys of seeing my daughter and her family, the best part of these visits has been being chauffeured around and doing a minimum of housework. Overall, I will fly again in the future!

Senior Citizens Center

I joined our city's senior citizens center about two years ago. This has been a lot of enjoyment meeting other senior citizens in the community. Most of the people who go there take advantage of the many activities offered at the center and participate in the available activities three to five days a week. With my other activities, I usually get to go only once or twice a week, but really feel welcome when I go. When I go, it is for lunch on Mondays and occasionally on Fridays. I have worked all day for the past two family fun fests that are held each fall on a Saturday. These are fun but make for a long day. Last year I participated in an event called "The Brain Games" which is a trivia contest among other senior centers in Middle Tennessee and will do so again this year. The center offers several day trips during the year. I took a lunch cruise on the *General Jackson*, which is a paddlewheel river boat that seats about 450 people for meals and is owned by the Gaylord Opryland Hotel in Nashville. I would encourage this kind of activity to anyone who has it available in your area.

I mentioned earlier in this book that I had my own business before I had my stroke. In fact the stress from the business was a real factor in causing my stroke. One part of the business that I really enjoyed, however, was the friendships I formed from joining our local Chamber of Commerce. Without having a business to promote any longer, though, there was no sense in maintaining my membership, and I had actually dropped it before my stroke. I still maintained a few friendships, and after two years of my stroke recovery, I went to an event that was a private car collection showing. The event was sponsored by the local Rotary Club as a fundraiser for a totally inclusive park for disabled children and adults. I had been to this collection for a private showing once before, but this was the first time I had been there when the owner opened it to the public. There were literally hundreds of people there seeing one of the best private auto collections in the country.

Rotary

While I was at this event, I saw an old friend from the Chamber. She was there alone, so we hung out together for the rest of the event. She kept introducing me to other Rotary members and encouraged me to join the club. Well, for two weeks I thought about it and finally decided to talk to her about what they all did, when they met, and, most importantly, what it would cost me. They do a lot of things that require physical effort, which I still can't do. On the other hand, there is quite a bit of brain-type stuff I can do. They meet at seven in the morning, and I am usually still in bed then. The cost really stretched my budget almost to the limit. No matter, I decided to go to a meeting to see what it was about. At the first meeting, I was welcomed by many of my pre-stroke friends and decided it was well worth joining. Since my first meeting almost three years ago, I haven't missed one.

I have been accepted at Rotary even with my physical disabilities. We have had really great speakers, such as the general manager of the Tennessee Titans football team and the governor of Tennessee. I went to all three training sessions for the Rotary Leadership Institute and recently went to meetings at the five other Rotary Clubs in our county. It's really neat to meet people who have been affected by the Rotary's work. One of the aphasia group's grad students, who was from Hendersonville (where I live), found out about my Rotary involvement. She was very appreciative of having been awarded a Rotary scholarship from our club for her undergraduate studies. I have to admit I was reluctant to go at first, but I am really glad

I joined this group. To be part of it is really meaningful, and I feel that it allows me to really do a lot of things for the good of our city.

My close personal relationships since my stroke have been essentially nonexistent. My third marriage ended a year before my stroke, and I was, quite frankly, too busy with my work to even consider dating. Over the recovery years, I concentrated on just plain getting better. While it is rewarding to participate in all that I do, it is also nice to get home and do as I please. If I want to read a book or watch something on TV, I can do it and not feel guilty about it. I went to bed when I wanted, got up when I wanted, and if I felt like going out to eat, I did; if not, I did-n't. Overall, I was very happy. At sixty-seven years old, I just had no desire to have any really personal relationships.

A Lady Friend

Then I met an attractive lady ten years younger than I am. I saw her from time to time in group settings. She was on disability from her nursing career due to health issues and had recently moved to town to be with her daughter and her family. One day we had lunch with a group of people, and she was lamenting about missing her work. That afternoon I had a stroke support group meeting and thought she might enjoy going. So I asked her if she would go and she agreed to. We had a decent time, and on the way back she indicated that she really didn't know her way around the city and didn't know what to do or where to go. Her daughter and son-in-law spent their time in Nashville when they went out, and that was too stressful for her. I told her that I very seldom went to Nashville because Hendersonville had so much to offer. This turned into a few dates, and eventually into evenings at my apartment watching movies or TV. We would take turns cooking, and we impressed each other with our cooking abilities. Eventually, she would spend some weekends here when we would go to a play or watch a late movie.

After we had been dating about five months, she had a major argument with her son-in-law. By then our relationship was strong enough that I suggested she move in with me. We shared our housework, went shopping together, and shared the cooking. We went out twice or more a week as well. We even planned a long weekend away and made hotel reservations and booked a couple of activities. After a few weeks, she began expressing her wishes that she could somehow get back to work so that we could take trips a few times a year. I suggested that she call the local Social Security office and find out if she could work and how much she could earn without jeopardizing her disability. Afterward, she found a suitable job that would not affect her disability and was happier. She opened a savings account to save her extra income.

Her daughter was spending more time here, and they went shopping together quite often. She had also made contact with her brothers that she hadn't seen or heard from in years. One brother was actually living in Nashville and another about two hours away in Kentucky. She also made contact with her extended family through one of her brothers. Things were going very well for her, and seemingly for us as well. She and I had lived together for about two and a half months.

Then one Sunday night after we had gone to bed about 11 P.M., I got up at 2:30 to use the bathroom. She was not in the bed. After I went to the bathroom, I checked to see if she was in the living room. Instead, I found a note on my desk with her apartment key. All of her things were gone. I was heartbroken, and it took me quite a while to get over her departure. I still think about her at least once a day. We had a really great time while it lasted.

Our relationship at least showed me that it was possible to have a relationship even after having a stroke. We had more than seven great months together and did many wonderful things. In the end, I am sure it wasn't meant to be for one reason or another. It took me a couple of weeks to get my apartment rearranged and it is ultimately, in a small part, better arranged than before she moved in. I could and do look at that as a benefit to having our friendship.

The items I wrote about here only scratch the surface of what is possible. Keep in mind that I still have a difficult time walking at anything near a normal pace and that my right arm and hand have about 10 percent of the function I had before my stroke. Even with these handicaps, and nearly seven years after my stroke, I am continuing to see improvements in my long-term recovery, and these changes continue to build my confidence.

In the first chapter of this book I said that I had two thoughts while I was in the hospital. The first was that God told me that I needed a vacation from working so hard. He has done just that, although it is a bit of an extended vacation. The second day, I decided to change my career from one of a sales orientation to a stroke recovery orientation. As you have read this book, I hope that I have shown that there is hope for most of us after having a stroke.

I've gone from seeing floors as having the surface irregularities of the Rocky Mountains when trying to move about unaided in a wheelchair to being a contributing part of several rather prominent service groups in my extended community. All of these activities are with very limited financial resources and with pretty limited physical abilities. Not everyone is going to be able to do or even want to do all that I have accomplished, but the ideas I have presented in this book are here to show you what *can* be done if you put your mind to it.

Henry Ford has been quoted as saying, "Whether you think you can or think you can't, you will be right." I prefer to think I *can* do things.

About
the Author

AUTHOR MIKE DOSEMAGEN HAS AN A.D. IN AUTOMOTIVE TECHNOLOGY AND A B.A. IN HUMAN RELATIONS MANAGEMENT. His work history includes twenty-seven years as a corporate quality manager in the auto and furniture industries and twelve years in sales, leading up to becoming the sales manager of the year at one company during his second year there. Dosemagen has no formal education in any medical field.

When he wrote this book, he wanted to put the basic things that he had experienced and learned into a simple format to help other stroke survivors get their full life back. He learned to LIVE A FULL LIFE again with his disabilities.

29444053R00148

Made in the USA
Lexington, KY
30 January 2019